Free & Bad Company
in the 1970s

John Van der Kiste

SONICBOND

sonicbondpublishing.com

Sonicbond Publishing Limited
www.sonicbondpublishing.co.uk
Email: info@sonicbondpublishing.co.uk

First Published in the United Kingdom 2022
First Published in the United States 2022

British Library Cataloguing in Publication Data:
A Catalogue record for this book is available from the British Library

ISBN 978-1-78952-178-8

Typeset in ITC Garamond & ITC Avant Garde
Printed and bound in England

Graphic design and typesetting: Full Moon Media

DECADES

Free & Bad Company in the 1970s

John Van der Kiste

SONICBOND

sonicbondpublishing.com

Acknowledgements

My thanks go to Paul Clayton of the Free Appreciation Society, and joint author – with Todd K. Smith – of the ultimate Free biography *Free: Heavy Load*, for his constant help, advice and willingness to answer my endless questions about the band; Kev Hunter, for his assistance with supplying material from his collection; my wife Kim, who has as ever been an unfailing support during my writing and research; and last but not least, to my ever-supportive publisher Stephen Lambe and the editorial team at Sonicbond.

DECADES | Free & Bad Company in the 1970s

Contents

Introduction

Free rose like a firework and fell back to earth almost as quickly. The last great name to come out of the British blues scene in 1968, two years later, they seemed to have the world at their feet and were hailed by the media as 'the new Rolling Stones'. A year after that, they had disintegrated, only to reform half-heartedly and evaporate for good almost as soon. Their vocalist and drummer – the two most-driven members – drew a line under the past and formed Bad Company: a band that learned from Free's mistakes and proved they were built to last, albeit with the odd hiatus or two. Between them, both bands left behind a catalogue of albums and singles that still sell and are much played half a century later. In particular, fans and fellow vocalists have long acclaimed frontman Paul Rodgers as possessing one of the finest voices in rock history: a singer equally at home with blues, hard rock and soul, and a versatile musician who has released solo albums on which he played every instrument.

The story of Free and Bad Company between them spans several decades, but the 1970s were their glory years. This is the tale and the music.

Chapter One: 1968–69

From the mid-1950s onwards, popular music in Britain underwent a remarkable transformation, and scarcely any young musician working during the next couple of decades remained unaffected. Maybe it was coincidence, maybe not, that while Bill Haley and his Comets and Elvis Presley were releasing their first 78 rpm (soon to be 45 rpm) singles, British labels became aware of the demand for American jazz, blues and skiffle music. Teenagers and young adults were not merely content to listen to rock 'n' roll, blues or skiffle, but also wanted to try their hand at playing the music themselves and forming their own bands. Chris Barber's Jazz Band, his protégé Lonnie Donegan, Alexis Korner, John Mayall, Cyril Davies and Wally Whyton all became prominent figures – if not founding fathers – of the burgeoning new music in one way or another. A bunch of Liverpool teenagers formed The Quarrymen in 1956, later morphing into The Beatles, with many others following in their train. The dividing lines between jazz, blues, skiffle, rock 'n' roll and R&B became increasingly indistinct as singers and musicians served brief apprenticeships with different revolving-door outfits and then formed their own bands. By the end of 1963, The Rolling Stones, The Mann-Hugg Blues Brothers (later Manfred Mann), The Animals and The Yardbirds were all on the verge of success with major hit singles. As some of them gravitated towards the pop market, others formed their own bands that stayed closer to the blues. Foremost among them were Cream, Peter Green's Fleetwood Mac, Chicken Shack, the trio who would become The Jimi Hendrix Experience (a British rhythm section fronted by an expatriate American guitarist in London), a little later Led Zeppelin, and a few months before them, Free.

The last-named appeared just as the British blues boom was drawing to a close. All four members had some experience with bands or other musicians during their teens. Paul Kossoff was only 15 when he discovered his true vocation after attending a gig by John Mayall's Bluesbreakers with Eric Clapton on guitar. A few months later – following several uninspiring day jobs – he found a more congenial post at Selmer's Music Store in Charing Cross Road. One day, a wiry-looking black guitarist entered the shop with his manager Chas Chandler: former bassist with The Animals. Though the guitarist didn't buy anything, everyone looked on in disbelief as he played a right-handed guitar upside down, and did so remarkably well. This was said to be Jimi Hendrix's first public performance anywhere in London. Paul was 16 when he joined the blues band Black Cat Bones in 1966, and they often played with veteran New Orleans blues singer and pianist, Champion Jack Dupree, as well as sometimes supporting Peter Green's Fleetwood Mac.

About a year later, Simon Kirke – an aspiring drummer who had come from Shropshire to London in the hope of making it as a musician – saw an ad in *Melody Maker* for a Champion Jack Dupree and Black Cat Bones gig at the Nag's Head pub in Battersea, and went to see them. He thought their drummer was hopeless, but was impressed with the guitarist Paul Kossoff. In the interval, they struck up a conversation at the bar, and Simon learned that the drummer was leaving and they were about to hold auditions to replace him. When Simon admitted he didn't have any drums, he was told that would not be a problem. He proved himself to be better than the competition, and duly joined the band.

Meanwhile, Paul Rodgers – born in Middlesbrough – had come down to London with his band – initially The Roadrunners but by now The Wildflowers as they thought the name suited the general flower-power ambience of the day. Among other members at various times were Micky Moody – later guitarist with Juicy Lucy and then Whitesnake – and Bruce Thomas: future bassist with Elvis Costello and The Attractions. Like almost every child of his generation, Paul had grown up in a household where the radio was constantly on, and was introduced to the music of Frank Sinatra, Elvis Presley, The Beatles and The Rolling Stones, all of which led him on a musical journey to B.B. King, Muddy Waters and Otis Redding. On joining the band, Paul played bass but was persuaded to relinquish it and front the band as singer instead as he had such a distinctive voice. Colin Bradley originally had the lead vocal slot but convinced Rodgers *he* ought to sing and front the band instead, as Colin really wanted to play rhythm guitar.

After moving to London, The Wildflowers fell apart. A *Melody Maker* ad seeking a vocalist for a blues band brought Paul to a combo that was also looking for a name, and he suggested they should call themselves Brown Sugar. Revealing himself to be not only a powerful singer and frontman, he also impressed them with his harmonica skills.

Bookings were coming in thick and fast, but none of the other members wanted to leave their steady day jobs and make music a full-time career. This was Paul's aim, and one night while they were playing at the Fickle Pickle in Finsbury Park, Paul Kossoff saw them. Their paths had already crossed briefly. They got chatting during the break, decided they wanted to create something new together and move on from their present bands, and the idea of a new outfit altogether – comprising both Pauls and Simon Kirke – began to take shape.

At around the same time, Andy Fraser – a teenage amateur guitarist, pianist and bassist – enrolled at Hammersmith Art College, where he befriended Sappho Korner. Her father was Alexis Korner, who became a kind of father figure to Andy. Alexis – one of the seminal figures of the British blues scene in the early 1960s – knew or had connections with almost everybody in the London blues scene. When 15-year-old Andy found a brief gig as bassist with John Mayall's Bluesbreakers, but was then given notice as John wanted to shift the band emphasis from blues to jazz, Andy was left high and dry. It was largely Mike Vernon – a club owner and founder of Blue Horizon: a blues label distributed by CBS and, at the time, home to Fleetwood Mac – who came to his rescue. He knew the trio of Paul Kossoff, Paul Rodgers and Simon Kirke needed a bass player, and asked Alexis if he knew anybody suitable. Alexis immediately recommended Andy.

There are at least two different accounts of what happened next and in what order. What's beyond doubt is that on the afternoon of 19 April 1968, Mike Vernon met Paul Kossoff at the Nag's Head pub in Battersea to unlock the doors of his club where they were going to rehearse. Simon Kirke and Paul Rodgers arrived by bus a little later, followed closely by Andy Fraser in a black cab. As he got out, everyone noticed that he asked the driver for a receipt. As they observed, he had already played with a big-name band, and with that kind of experience, he clearly knew what he was doing. At the jam session that followed, Paul Rodgers would call out the titles of various blues standards and they would play away. The great thing about blues, he said, was 'you can all jam on it and you find out how good everybody is because you've already got the structure, the 12-bar thing'. All afternoon the music kept going, and they even wrote a couple of songs. Simon later claimed that when they came to record their first album a few months later, about half of it had been written or rehearsed during those few hours. The creative spirit went hand in hand with a sense of adventure. Alexis – who was celebrating his 40th birthday that same day – walked in during the session with family members. After they had listened appreciatively and applauded, Alexis phoned up booking agent Bryan Morrison and told him he ought to come down and see them, as something very special was going on.

After the band put down their instruments, they sat down and discussed where and how to proceed. Andy immediately said he would be their leader. They immediately thought that it was rather pompous of him, as he was the youngest. However, they thought if he really had what it takes, they might as well let him have a go. Alexis was still there, and when the subject turned to a band name, he said he'd previously played in a band with Graham Bond and Ginger Baker called Free At Last. Free on its own would be perfect. A simple one-word name had worked for acts like Cream and Traffic, and they all agreed.

Koss and Simon already had their recording debut lined up. Mike Vernon had asked them to play on an album he was overseeing for Champion Jack Dupree – *When You Feel the Feeling You Was Feeling* – alongside Black Cat Bones bassist Stuart Brooks and harmonica player Duster Bennett. They recorded eight tracks in about three hours, with five being used on the album, another on a subsequent single, and two remaining in the vaults. They then fulfilled their final obligation to Mike Vernon by supporting Fleetwood Mac at the Marquee on 26 April.

Free were now ready to start gigging. Alexis told everybody he met that they were going to be huge, and in order to give the band some experience and wider exposure, he took them on tour with him. Playing in small clubs and concert venues gave them the opportunity to hone their skills from the rough-and-ready early shows and gradually improve. He would give them a generous build-up as they took the stage for their own set, and then do his own solo spot, bringing Free back on so they could close the show together. For a short time, Alexis co-managed Free with Bryan Morrison, and they played together at Rambling Jack's Blues Club at the Railway Hotel, Bishop's Stortford, and at Middle Earth, Covent Garden, sharing a bill with Pink Floyd.

Simon later reminisced that at the start, 'the chemistry was just right'. Having been released from the restraints of their previous groups, they were ready to forge ahead. Koss and Simon contributed to the songs, but it was soon evident that Paul Rodgers and Andy were going to be their Lennon-McCartney; their Jagger-Richards: a ready-made song factory, writing up to 15 songs a week, then going through them and discarding the ones that didn't work. Alexis was very impressed with their ability to come up with so much original material and not needing to rely on the standards that so many other young bands were churning out.

For a while, they used Andy's mother's house in Roehampton as a base to meet regularly, sometimes bringing favourite albums for a listening session. Early Rolling Stones, Otis Redding, Isaac Hayes or The Beatles' *Revolver* were usually on the turntable. One night they sat up into the early hours, writing letters to club promoters in pursuit of further bookings. Very few answered back, and most who did said they thought the name Free was too arty and that punters might take it the wrong way by thinking any advertising for the band would mean free admission. Significantly, once Free began playing live, tickets and publicity sometimes printed their name as 'The Free'.

Andy soon proved he had a surprisingly good business head on his young shoulders. He worked painstakingly with Bryan Morrison, taking care of financial and business matters, bookkeeping and securing more gigs. Bryan provided some money for them to record a few demos, and a month later, began complaining about the band's expenses. As Andy was meticulous about their working and living within their means with no unnecessary outlay, it took them all by surprise. Relations between Bryan and the band rapidly deteriorated, coming to an end when he angrily threw them a cheque and said there would be no more, so they'd better make it last. It made little difference as their contract had only been for six months and was up for review anyway.

Soon afterwards, they met the head of Island Records, Chris Blackwell. Having founded the label in Jamaica and found there was keen interest in the reggae, ska and R&B singles he was issuing in Britain, he opened an office in London. His records were originally issued on Philips' subsidiary label Fontana, but in 1967 it became a separate entity when the newly formed Traffic was signed. Within a couple of years, Island acquired a formidable roster of talent outside the mainstream pop market, including Fairport Convention, Jethro Tull, Nick Drake, Spooky Tooth, Mott The Hoople and King Crimson.

It was probably Alexis who introduced Free to Chris, though some said he became interested after seeing Free at the Marquee and thought they reminded him of a younger Small Faces. As a result, he arranged a showcase gig for them at Studio 512 – a rehearsal room at Leicester Square – bringing along three of the Island management team: John Glover, Alec Leslie and Muff Winwood (elder brother of Steve). All three of them were distinctly unimpressed, but Chris overruled them and insisted on signing them. At a private meeting between band and record-company staff, the band told them they were 'the best thing' they had, and would sooner walk out of the room than take second place to anybody. Glover thought they were being particularly aggressive and overconfident in that the four untried and untested teenage nobodies looking for their first record deal were trying to lay down the law in the managers' office before they'd barely started. Perhaps fortunately for them, Bryan Morrison was having financial difficulties and was keen to ease his cash flow by letting Island buy them out for a pittance. He and Chris came to an arrangement and offered Free a six-month contract – a normal deal for the time – with a review option for possible extension at the end of the term.

The first item on his agenda was to give them a more marketable name. Management and Island's main producer Guy Stevens disliked the idea of calling them Free. Muff Winwood said he'd seen them at the Marquee, thought they sounded good and was keen to give them a management and recording contract, but Free sounded 'too nebulous'. They suggested it should be changed to The Heavy Metal Kids, after a street gang in a William S. Burroughs novel. The band thought that was a dreadful idea, and on behalf of them all, Andy said if they really wanted to sign them, the name was Free, so take it or leave it. The meeting ended in a stalemate with neither side prepared to concede. All four members left, convinced they'd just shot themselves in the foot. Returning to Andy's home, they wrote both names on separate cards, placed them on the mantelpiece and decided to stick to their guns. Andy then rang Blackwell and said they had no intention of changing their name. Blackwell replied, 'Sorry, no deal then,' and hung up. Five minutes later, he called them back, told them they would drop The Heavy Metal Kids idea and accept the band's decision. They had won their first battle. (Another band – fronted by actor/singer Gary Holton – adopted The Heavy Metal Kids moniker five years later.)

On 15 July – between further gigs at the Marquee, Bishop's Stortford and elsewhere – they recorded an audition-cum-session for BBC Radio 1 in the studio at Piccadilly. Four of their originals – 'Waiting On You', 'Walk In My Shadow', 'Free Me' and 'Moonshine' – were taped, and John Peel broadcast them on *Top Gear* six days later. For Simon and Koss – if not for all four – it was one of the greatest moments of their lives as they huddled around a radio that afternoon to listen. Though they were critical of their performance – saying 'it was too slow' or 'we should've done this' – it was still an important achievement. By the time Peel announced afterwards that he was sure they would be hearing a lot more of the band, they were over the moon.

Further gigs over the next few months helped to build up a following, and with experience, they knew they were improving, becoming tighter all the time. In September, they were on the bill for the 1st National Blues Convention at Conway Hall in Red Lion Square, London, alongside

Champion Jack Dupree and his new outfit Dynaflow Blues, Aynsley Dunbar's Retaliation and Duster Bennett, with compères Alexis Korner and Radio 1 presenter Mike Raven. Though still in their teens, Free were the ultimate professionals – dedicated to and focused on their work. Andy was the multi-instrumentalist: a bassist who'd already mastered piano and knew his way around a Mellotron. He also had a good business head – working hand in glove with Island management, collecting the cash for gigs, sharing it out between band and company as agreed, while banking additional funds to cover tax, equipment and van repairs. He had a kindred spirit in Paul Rodgers, who insisted they adopt a policy of total professionalism, with no distractions of outside jobs, and working weekdays and weekends. Local promoters were impressed with their dedication – their turning up early to gigs, going straight to the dressing room, playing their hearts out until they were fired up to go onstage and ready to give their best, regardless of how many or few might be in the audience.

In October, Free entered Morgan Studios to record the cream of their regular live set more or less live in the studio. Guy Stevens was designated as producer, with Andy Johns as engineer. With them came Steve Miller – a British blues piano player whom they met when he played with his own band at Bishop's Stortford; Free making a mental note that he would be an ideal guest musician if the opportunity arose. The sessions took about six days, spread throughout the month, and proved to be relatively straightforward. Most of the taped songs went on the first album, with the exception of 'Free Me', which was held back until next time; 'Woman by the Sea', which they rejected, only to use the lyrics in another song on a subsequent album; 'Remember', 'Visions Of Hell' and the impromptu blues jam 'Guy Stevens Blues', which likewise remained in the archives. A fragment listed on the multitrack box as 'Muck About' was actually 'Long Tall Sally' minus the first minute or so, as Andy Johns evidently pressed the record button after they'd started playing. Master mixes were completed at the beginning of November.

Though Guy Stevens was credited as producer, his role was very much an abstract one. The man who once claimed there were only two Phil Spectors and he was one of them was renowned for motivating the groups he produced. His main role was to encourage them and exhort them to greater heights – like that of a sports coach standing on the edge of a playing field, urging them to do their best, and if possible, even better than that. Though he'd been an avid record collector for many years, he couldn't read or write music, play an instrument or sing a note to save his life. He loved rock music, R&B and soul. But as Andy Johns remarked, 'He didn't know an E string from a teapot.' Unlike other hands-on producers who would add extra vocals or instruments to a band's recorded work, his part in the process was abstract in the extreme. He was notoriously eccentric, but Chris Blackwell had great faith in him, letting him get away with almost anything – even deliberately setting fire to the studio in order to create atmosphere: something he later did with Mott The Hoople while producing their fourth album.

Paul Rodgers called Guy 'a mad genius' who never understood where they were coming from. They were fully in touch with the street and what was going down in the clubs at the time, whereas his guiding principle was 'a kind of zany commerciality' or strange psychedelia that they avoided because it was not the blues. He wanted to call one of their songs on the first album 'The Cabbages Of My Mind', which would've been fine for an act like The Bonzo Dog Band, but Paul told him he must be joking. Nevertheless, Guy did supply the album title *Tons Of Sobs* – 'sob' or 'sov' being slang for a pound, or as others would have it: another term for delta blues wailing.

Another interesting idea Guy may have been responsible for was vehemently denied by Andy Johns, who always maintained that he and not Guy had thought of it – which was to cut the one acoustic track 'Over The Green Hills' into two sections, placing one at the beginning of side one and the other at the end of side two, cross-fading them with the adjacent numbers to provide something of a contrast to the raw electric blues tone of the rest.

Apart from that, the album was a faithful snapshot of how they sounded onstage, though devoid of the immediacy that comes across when performing to an audience. Having almost no previous studio experience, Free knew nothing about all the bells and whistles available to enhance the sound if they wanted them, and were dependent on the superior technical knowledge of their producer (in Guy's case, amounting to zero) and engineer. It is interesting to consider that Led Zeppelin – Britain's other great new blues-rock contemporaries – were in another London studio nearby at the same time, recording their debut album to be released in America in January 1969 and Britain in March. Yet their guitarist and producer Jimmy Page was already an experienced veteran with a vast history of sessions for other artists. In comparison, Free were comparative youngsters, still at the starting gate. (Fifteen years on, Paul Rodgers and Jimmy Page were to collaborate: a story for later.)

Recording their debut album was an exciting experience for Free in theory, but in practice, not an enjoyable one. Paul Rodgers loved performing in front of an audience, and he found the environment at Morgan (or any other studio) hygienic, antiseptic and devoid of any kind of atmosphere. He hated the bright lights and tried to get the right mood by turning them down, closing his eyes and trying hard to imagine he was onstage. The very idea of putting a vocalist in an airless cupboard in order to get a better sound, he said, was astonishing. For him, that was the negative side of recording, to be vindicated to some extent when he returned home to Middlesbrough with a test pressing of the completed album under his arm.

Most of the record – which Simon called 'essentially a blues album with more adventurous leanings' – was recorded during several days in October and mixed at the beginning of November. The original song 'Visions Of Hell' was removed from the running order before release. According to Paul Rodgers, it was an experimental number that he and Andy had written, with a very unorthodox verse/chorus structure, so Guy advised them to drop it 'because it was so weird'. He told them to replace it with the song that had proven to be something of an anthem onstage and always went down well – their no-holds-barred version of Booker T. and the M.G.'s' 'The Hunter', recorded by Albert King the previous year. This was one instance where Paul Rodgers later remembered several lead guitar overdubs, supplied by Koss. When asked about the album years later, Paul recalled being told he could redo his original vocal, but couldn't remember whether he did or not.

Once they added this song to their set, it remained the one they could never omit. From the early days – after he'd written 'Walk In My Shadow' and 'Over The Green Hills' – Paul told them it would be in their interests to phase out the blues cover versions and replace 'The Hunter' with as much original material as possible, as it would give them an identity. Nevertheless, the song stayed as they swore they could never write anything better, and it became the right closing number.

While the debut album was in the can awaiting sleeve design and release, they went back on the road on a package tour with The Who, Small Faces and recent chart-toppers Joe Cocker and The Crazy World Of Arthur Brown. In mid-November, it was followed by another session for the BBC for which they played four songs on *Rhythm & Blues*: presented by Alexis Korner, to be broadcast in December on the BBC World Service.

Free: Tons Of Sobs *(1969)*

Personnel:
Paul Rodgers: vocals
Paul Kossoff: guitar
Andy Fraser: bass, piano
Simon Kirke: drums
Additional personnel:
Steve Miller: piano
Producer: Guy Stevens
Recorded at Morgan Studios, Willesden, October–December 1968
Engineer: Andy Johns
Release date: March 1969
Chart placing: US: 197
Running time: 38:55
Side One: 1. Over The Green Hills (Pt. 1) (Rodgers) 2. Worry (Rodgers) 3. Walk In My Shadow (Rodgers, Kossoff, Fraser, Kirke) 4. Wild Indian Woman (Rodgers, Fraser) 5. Goin' Down Slow (James Burke Oden)
Side Two: 1. I'm A Mover (Rodgers, Fraser) 2. The Hunter (Booker T. Jones, Carl Wells, Donald Dunn, Al Jackson Jr., Steve Cropper) 3. Moonshine (Rodgers, Kossoff, Fraser, Kirke) 4. Sweet Tooth (Rodgers) 5. Over The Green Hills (Pt. 2) (Rodgers)
Bonus tracks on CD remastered reissue 2001: I'm A Mover (BBC session) (Rodgers / Fraser), Waitin' On You (BBC session) (B.B. King / Ferdinand Washington), Guy Stevens Blues (Rodgers / Kossoff / Fraser / Kirke), Moonshine (Alternative vocal) (Rodgers / Kossoff / Fraser / Kirke), Sweet Tooth (Early take and alternative vocal) (Rodgers), Visions Of Hell (Rodgers / Fraser), Woman By The Sea (Rodgers / Fraser), Over The Green Hills (BBC session) (Rodgers)

The opening notes of Free's debut album act as a kind of unexpected overture: a 50-second fragment of 'Over The Green Hills'. Though uncredited at the time, Simon played acoustic guitar on the track. It cross-fades spectacularly well into 'Worry', with its gritty, rumbling guitar track and Steve Miller's piano fleshing out the overall sound, behind a brooding lyric that sings of 'The cold black night that's eating up your heart'.

'Walk In My Shadow' is a song Paul Rodgers had begun and played with Brown Sugar. He said later that it was the first he'd ever written himself, and it started when they were playing a riff and he began singing over it, making up words as he went along. When they told him it was an old blues riff, he decided they couldn't use it, so he wrote a 12-bar blues around the framework, and took the song from there. When he brought it to Free, they developed it together and ended up with a four-way collaboration – a song that was basically 12-bar blues, with a rather macho lyric ('When I get you in the shadow/I'm gonna lay you on the floor') spiced up with some sturdy guitar riffs. It's one of the few songs without piano on the album.

'Wild Indian Woman' is another mid-tempo blues track with vigorous riffing and guitar licks curling around the lines, accompanying another self-assured, mildly sexist lyric that might have incurred some disapproval in a later age: 'You don't need your horses, babe, you got me to ride/ You don't need your feathers, I'll keep you warm inside'. The guitar solo, with piano in the background, is a masterclass in note economy for effect, proving that sometimes less is more.

At almost nine minutes in length – the longest track Free ever recorded – 'Goin' Down Slow' is one of only two cover versions on the album: a blues number written and first recorded by Chicago singer St. Louis Jimmy Oden in the early 1940s. The deathbed lament of a man who knows he's paying for a life of self-indulgence, asking for forgiveness from his mother if he never recovers, it was also later recorded by Bobby Bland and Howlin' Wolf. In keeping with the title, Paul Rodgers slows it down as he wrings every little bit of drama from the lyric, Kossoff's anguished guitar licks filling in the spaces, and Miller's rippling jazz piano runs adding to the colour.

Opening with some neat drum fills, and punctuated with raw, punchy guitar licks against a sturdy bass riff, 'I'm A Mover' is the song of a restless spirit – a man who was born by the river and has been moving ever since, even forsaking his wife and 11 children.

Last-minute addition 'The Hunter' follows in all its glory, the tone set by one of Kossoff's most powerful guitar intros ever. (Coincidentally, Led Zeppelin also recorded it around the same time on their first album: integrated into the lengthy 'How Many More Times'.) Later, critics often used songs like this – in a derogatory sense – against hard rock bands, in wilful ignorance of the fact that it was no more than a tradition that could be traced back to original blues performers around 30 years earlier.

Although it ended up as a four-way credit, 'Moonshine' was developed from a Kossoff riff after he asked Paul Rodgers to produce some lyrics that complemented the dark mood he was trying to convey. The result is a downbeat, brooding song in the Robert Johnson tradition; a 12-bar of sorts – 'Sitting in a graveyard, waiting for the dawn/Leaning on my gravestone till the night has gone'. The sustained guitar notes help perpetuate an almost surreal mood.

The final complete song – 'Sweet Tooth' – is based on a simple riff punctuated by fuzztone guitar chords. It's a relatively commercial song with a bluesy backbone. Guitars and drums sustain the vocal section well, with Miller's piano only coming in after the final chorus as the guitar lines shimmer and flow towards a closing frenzy and dramatic drums sign-off, giving way to the concluding fragment of 'Over The Green Hills'.

A self-assured debut, the album is the sound of a group who evidently matured into the blues surprisingly fast. All three musicians are solid players, while Paul Rodgers' vocals are full-blooded one moment, suitably restrained the next. While there seems to be no consensus among fans as to which was the best Free album of all, this one has always been one of their best-regarded.

Like the title, the sleeve design was, in large measure, another creation of their producer. Guy conceived the idea, perhaps inspired by the lyrics of 'Moonshine'. The photograph – taken in a graveyard in the Putney and Barnes area of south-west London – shows a doom-laden scene of a huge Plexiglas coffin containing a model of Mickey Mouse, with a leopard stalking a rabbit nearby.

In the first week of January 1969, Free returned to the studio to record 'Broad Daylight', which was released as a single in March, with 'The Worm' on the B-side. Both were Rodgers-Fraser compositions. This shifting of the centre of creative gravity towards the singer and bassist as the group's Lennon-McCartney ill-suited Koss, who found himself increasingly marginalised. On the first album he'd been content to contribute his own guitar lead lines, but in future sessions, he found they required him to play more rhythm and less lead, and he'd never regarded the former as his strongest point. Andy Fraser was not only co-writing the songs, but increasingly arranging them, also dispensing with outside keyboard players and adding piano and organ parts himself; later Mellotron, when required.

The partnership between Andy and Paul Rodgers flourished, Paul's strength, as vocalist, being naturally on the lyrics, to which Andy would initially devise arrangements, and between them they would work on the melody. Some songs originated with the vocalist writing a song in rough form, and taking it to rehearsal, when Andy would rearrange the basic idea and develop it for the group. Others came about through Andy coming up with the music and basic backing track, with Paul then adding lyrics. An alternative way was for them to enter the studio with nothing, and someone would start knocking out a riff or a melody, they'd 'mess about with it', and later that day or evening they'd end up with another new number more or less complete. At the same time, Paul was developing his guitar skills: playing mostly rhythm, but beginning to try his hand at basic lead. It gave them an additional strength that would soon become useful and even necessary at times.

The 'Broad Daylight' single hit the shops around the same time as *Tons of Sobs*. Both received good reviews, but the former was ignored by radio and neither of them sold strongly enough to make the charts. Even so, the group continued to build themselves a following through regular gigs around England, particularly in Sunderland and the North East. Another BBC Radio 1 session – consisting of four songs – was recorded at the Playhouse Theatre, London, and broadcast on John Peel's *Top Gear* a week later, with a short spot for BBC TV's *Colour Me Pop* the following month, and another for Alexis Korner's *Rhythm & Blues* show on the World Service in May.

That same summer, sessions began in earnest for a second album. By then, band relations had come under some strain, with Koss increasingly resentful of Andy telling him what to play, even to the extent of their sitting down together so that Andy could more or less teach him the precise parts he wanted on the songs. Whereas the first album had been wrapped up in a few days – more or less putting their live performance down onstage with the minimum of frills – Andy's increasing perfectionism was beginning to grate on the others, Paul Kossoff and Simon in particular. It was of less concern to Paul Rodgers, who broadly shared Andy's views. Moreover, the example of others was not lost on Paul: that they needed to phase out most of the blues standards and replace them with their material. He'd learned that the writing partnership in any band stood to gain by far the most when it came – as it surely would – to hit singles, albums and subsequent royalty revenue. 'The Hunter' and 'Crossroads' had become live staples, and would remain that way. But that aside, the rest had to go. In time he would have a change of heart, admitting that he missed playing the blues that had initially brought them together. But at this point in time, he was convinced they had no option but to write and perform their own.

Guy Stevens had been scheduled to produce again, and he thought the band might be on the verge of imploding. Thinking Andy was about to leave (or, as has been suggested, planning to find someone more amenable to replace him and then tell him he was sacked), Guy placed an ad in *Melody Maker* for a 'tough, aggressive bass player'. Among those who answered was Pete Overend Watts, then playing with a band called Silence. He came with the understanding that Paul Kossoff and Simon Kirke were looking for a new member – perhaps two – to replace Andy and Paul, who were on the point of departing. Having done his homework by learning their single 'Broad Daylight', Pete went along with Silence guitarist Mick Ralphs for moral support, and ended up jamming on a few 12-bar blues with the drummer and lead guitarist. The audition led to nothing in one respect, in that the two members who'd been thought likely to depart were persuaded back to the fold. Nevertheless, Pete and Mick used their connection with Guy Stevens to obtain an audition that led to Silence signing to Island shortly afterwards, and changing their name to Mott The Hoople.

Andy and Paul knew nothing of the ad or the audition until a long time afterwards. Word had got to Chris Blackwell that they were thinking of walking, though both of them later denied it had reached that stage. Recollections vary, with Paul Rodgers later emphatically saying Guy Stevens was never in a position to audition anybody for a job 'in my band'. Whatever the truth of the matter, whether a *coup d'état* led by Island management in league with the guitarist and drummer was being launched to fire the other two, or whether it was just the standard but easy soluble disagreement between four equals, is anyone's guess. Paul Kossoff was feeling disenchanted enough to secretly audition for guitarist vacancies with Jethro Tull, and The Rolling Stones after Brian Jones was asked to leave.

Nevertheless, by summer it was business as usual when they were back in Morgan and Trident Studios, working on the second album. Blackwell was convinced that if they released the right track, they could have a hit on their hands, especially as he feared he'd lost one of his brightest hopes when Steve Winwood left Traffic a few months earlier (only temporarily, it transpired) to help form the ill-fated supergroup Blind Faith.

One of the first completed numbers from the new Free sessions was 'I'll Be Creepin'': issued as a 45 at the end of the month, though it fared no better than its predecessor. The opening line 'If you're tryin' to screw me baby', allegedly did not go down well with the ever-cautious BBC Radio 1 playlist panel.

Once Island had signed Mott The Hoople, Guy Stevens mainly devoted his attention to them. He was a notoriously volatile character, and Blackwell may have realised that to put him in charge of Free was not ideal. Knowing the band's internal relationships were fragile at best, and they could suddenly crumble if not handled carefully, he oversaw the new album sessions himself: determined to exert his encouragement and diplomatic skills to the full. Simon was frustrated, while Paul Kossoff – whose sense of humour and ever-ready repartee belied an insecure and sensitive character – was losing confidence in himself and his ability, turning to alcohol and drugs. Andy Johns noticed that Kossoff would become so intense and wrapped up in his playing, he'd unwittingly pull faces, never comb his lion's mane of hair, and had become the butt of much joking and laughter: something he found more hurtful than he was prepared to admit.

Following time in the studio and a few more dates in England, Free departed for their first tour of America. Steve Winwood had recommended Free as an ideal support act for Blind Faith and Delaney & Bonnie and Friends, who'd been booked to play several dates in July and August. Before the schedule began in earnest, the band had a few days to recover from jet lag and play some small gigs as a kind of warm-up. At one New York City club, they supported Dr. John, and to their surprise, Eric Clapton and Ginger Baker of Blind Faith walked in and sat in a darkened corner so they could catch part of Free's set. After they finished, Paul Kossoff and Simon went to say hello. Paul was amazed when Eric asked him how he managed to get that vibrato when he played (his hero was actually asking *him* about his guitar technique) and was more than happy to give him a demonstration afterwards.

A few weeks later, near the end of the tour, both guitarists swapped instruments, with Paul acquiring a Les Paul Sunburst – said to be the one Eric had recorded most of Cream's classic *Disraeli Gears* album with two years earlier – and Eric, a black Les Paul Custom. While they were still in America, each Free member gathered that all was not well in the headlining quartet's camp, when Steve Winwood joined them briefly at a roadside hotel and told them he envied them their freedom to do what they wanted. None of them were surprised when Blind Faith fell apart in some disarray once the tour was finished.

Meanwhile, in mid-August, the Woodstock festival was staged in New York, with a strong line-up of established and new American and British artists. The organisers were seeking a few more little-known bands to fill gaps on the first and second day, and Free were invited. But any plans for them to play were nixed when their personal manager Johnny Glover told them it would mean a very long journey in appalling traffic. They would long rue the day they turned down the opportunity.

In the last week of August, *Tons Of Sobs* was released in America, and Free returned to their homeland, joining the bill at the Isle of Wight festival headlined by Bob Dylan & The Band, and including The Who, The Nice, Family and The Edgar Broughton Band. Due to bad organisation and poorly-adhered-to running times, Free were restricted to a 15-minute set, but defiantly managed to extend that by a further ten minutes. It was some compensation for being unable to play Woodstock. They found it very draining having to play to such a large crowd and came offstage exhausted, with no idea how reaction to their set had been as the audience seemed so far away. Nevertheless, they were told they had gone down well, and the press feedback was positive.

Free: Free (1969)

Personnel:
Paul Rodgers: vocals
Paul Kossoff: guitar
Andy Fraser: bass, piano, acoustic guitar
Simon Kirke: drums
Additional personnel:
Chris Wood: flute
Producer: Chris Blackwell
Engineer: Andy Johns
Recorded at Morgan Studios and Trident Studios, London, January–June 1969
Release date: 25 September 1969
Chart placing: US: 177
Running time: 35:56
All songs by Rodgers/Fraser unless stated otherwise
Side One: 1. I'll Be Creepin' 2. Songs Of Yesterday 3. Lying In The Sunshine 4. Trouble On Double Time (Rodgers, Fraser, Kossoff, Kirke) 5. Mouthful Of Grass
Side Two: 1. Woman 2. Free Me 3. Broad Daylight 4. Mourning Sad Morning
Bonus tracks on subsequent CD reissues: Broad Daylight (Single edit), The Worm, I'll Be Creepin' (Single edit), Sugar For Mr Morrison, Broad Daylight (BBC session), Songs Of Yesterday (BBC session), Mouthful Of Grass, Woman, Trouble On Double Time (Early version), Mourning Sad Morning

Unlike their debut album, the eponymous *Free* was not really one to be filed comfortably in the blues section of a record shop. A few listens to the music suggest a band that's looking towards expanding its palate into more folky, acoustic directions. Whereas Led Zeppelin were tempering their slow bluesy numbers and the occasional acoustic interlude of the first two albums with the killer-paced 'Communication Breakdown' and 'Whole Lotta Love', Free were relatively laid-back. This is a good, varied album, but heavy it certainly is not. At least one retrospective reviewer has remarked that there are perhaps ten or 15 seconds of hard rock to be heard, and no more, while at the time of release, *NME* – possibly under the illusion it was intended as a folk album – remarked, 'Paul Rodgers and the others sing wistfully together, and the whole LP is most-restful listening.'

Wisely, they chose one of the strongest tracks to start side one. 'I'll Be Creepin'' – already released as a single – opens with some distinctive wah-wah guitar and bass riffing, with Paul Rodgers' gutsy vocals being the icing on the cake. Paul evidently remained fond of the song, embarking on a solo career over 20 years later and playing a tour where the song opened the set.

'Songs Of Yesterday' – a title which in 2000 lent itself to a five-CD collection of largely unissued material – boasts some interesting tempo variations. It begins fairly fast, with hints of a more commercial pop-rock, moving to a slower, rolling bluesy mood and back again. Simon said it was a great favourite of theirs to play because of the change. The blues portions naturally give Koss every chance to shine on his instrument, and it features what's probably Andy's most inventive bass work on the album.

If ever a song was tailor-made for summer, 'Lying In The Sunshine' is the one. This is Free the almost-folk band, with Andy's intimate guitar playing so delicate that on the remaster the sound of squeaking fingers moving up the fretboard is clearly heard. With the restrained bass notes, a soft shuffle on the drums and ethereal vocal harmonies, this is Free like they were rarely heard before, or even since.

'Trouble On Double Time' is instantly enough to reassure anyone that it's the Free they already knew. A blast of gritty blues rock with catchy riffs leads to a first-rate Kossoff solo, with another tempo change slowing it down just before the end. It's the only track on the album to feature a four-way writing credit.

There's a reversion to folky restraint on 'Mouthful Of Grass'. Andy's acoustic guitar provides an instrumental with a tune similar to that of 'Sunshine', punctuated by exquisite runs from partway through, with sparing bass and no drums. Cavernous-sounding backing vocals reminiscent of songs like Simon & Garfunkel's 'The Only Living Boy In New York', enhance the mood.

The mood again switches abruptly for the beginning of side two. 'Woman' is another tough, gritty blues-based song, with lead and bass runs complementing each other well. A softer, more tender passage near the end adds a touch of variety. Like 'Creepin'', Paul Rodgers admitted it was written specifically for the stage.

One of two tracks that lasts over five minutes (the closing number is the other), 'Free Me' (originally recorded faster during the *Tons Of Sobs* sessions but discarded) is arguably the least inspired. A few seconds in, every Led Zeppelin fan will be thinking 'Dazed And Confused', and using that pattern as a hypnotic chant has a certain charm, but it continues throughout the vocal section and then with the guitar break. Adding a few seconds of a cappella singing near the end is a clever touch, but taken as a whole, basing almost the entire track round the same six-note pattern becomes samey and wears thin towards the end. A repetition of the 'Over The Green Hills' idea – slicing into parts one and two to begin and end – might've been the answer. Despite this, it was one of the band's favourites, and they introduced it thus onstage. In its favour, it should be noted that unlike Koss' contemporaries who competed for the fastest guitarist in town prize, he was noted for his tasteful, slow solos, and this is a good example.

For those who didn't buy it first as a single – and one assumes that means almost everyone – 'Broad Daylight' comes next. Rather slow, it's diminished by being so repetitive. Singing the title four times in succession to the same three notes does not an appealing, attention-grabbing chorus make. Koss' guitar solo is the redeeming feature, but the impression is of a song written in a hurry and not developed with much imagination.

'Mourning Sad Morning' restores the quality, even though again it's a relatively folky Free: perhaps their equivalent of the Stones' 'As Tears Go By' in fact. Just as melancholy in mood as the title implies, Paul Rodgers becomes Paul Simon as he sings of doleful reminiscences of better times, as if writing a letter to a former love. It does highlight the fact that the man much famed as a gruff, almost shouty blues singer was equally capable of committing a powerful ballad to tape, and this was one of the numbers that led him to describe the record as 'more a soul album'. Simon Kirke commented that Chris Blackwell was a great believer in Island groups interacting with each other, and it was doubtless at his suggestion that Chris Wood – temporarily left high and dry while Traffic were on hiatus – plays flute, the only other instrument on the song besides acoustic guitar.

While he didn't go along with the perception of some that it was partly an acoustic folk record, Paul Rodgers readily conceded that it was much more introspective than their first. He said he and Andy had tried to visualise the mechanics of the writing process as Lennon and McCartney used to. There was a huge difference between sitting at home in the living room or strumming an acoustic guitar around the campfire, and being onstage in front of a vast audience with electric guitars and all the amplifiers. Some of the new songs were written with the former ambience in mind, others for the latter. Simon – whose involvement in the writing process was minimal – agreed that album number two was 'a more sedate affair'. At the time and years later, some reviewers have dismissed what they call the more folky/psych songs, as boring, bland and unmemorable, while others have praised them as the work of a group who were exploring the boundaries and refusing to confine themselves to electric blues.

If the sleeve design for *Tons Of Sobs* had been odd, that of *Free* was striking, and over the years, would be much praised for its stylish photography, even appearing in some books of classic album art. It was based on a photograph taken by Ron Raffaelli, who worked in Hollywood, using as his model the 18-year-old Linda Blair (not the actress from *The Exorcist*) striding over him naked, the outline of her body filled with stars as if leaping through the skies. Inside the gatefold were several shots of her in the Mojave Desert, having apparently uncovered a collection of building blocks in the sand, four of them with pictures of the band members: faces, and blowing sand off the one of Paul Rodgers, as if blowing his mind. The others observed wryly that it was 'typical Paul' to be on the one that she was holding.

Despite the design's artistic qualities, it might not have aided the album's sales potential when the title (being both artist and album) appeared in minute letters at the top: small enough on vinyl and later almost invisible on CD, although admittedly, the latter problem could not have been foreseen in 1969. Yet how many would-be purchasers browsed through the album racks and overlooked it as they didn't see who the artist was?

Again, sales were modest and the record failed to chart. Even so, they continued to play gigs around the country, finding particularly receptive audiences at Sunderland Locarno (sometimes known unofficially as the Fillmore North), an area where they'd developed a strong following. Further sessions for BBC Radio 1 and the World Service followed. The band, Blackwell and the rest of the senior staff at Island Records were convinced that a breakthrough for Free was only a matter of time. As the

1960s drew to a close, the music press and broadcasting media – above all, Radio 1 with its *Sounds of the Seventies* showcase for what was still known as underground and progressive music – were keen to predict who would be the first major acts of the next decade, and Free featured highly on several people's lists.

Chapter Two: 1970

A few days into the new year and decade, a managerial decision was taken to record Free onstage for a subsequent live album. In-concert recordings were starting to circulate on bootleg vinyl albums, changing hands at large prices. The fact that they were strictly illegal made them more collectable still, but for the artists who didn't receive any royalties, were annoyed with the poor audio quality and felt their music was being presented in an unfavourable light, they were bad news. In January, Island brought the Pye mobile studio to record part of a show played before an ecstatic crowd at Sunderland, to be kept for release at a suitable time.

Most of the songs captured had appeared on the first two albums, but the Rodgers/Fraser team had constantly been hard at work coming up with new material to keep the live set fresh. Among the most recent additions to the repertoire were four that would feature on the third album, and were gradually beginning to take shape – 'Mr Big', 'Remember' and 'Oh I Wept'. The one that was about to transform their standing at a stroke was 'All Right Now'.

The saga of how the song came about depends on whose version is considered the most accurate. According to Simon, they came offstage after one dreadful gig in the north – probably around the closing few weeks of 1969 – to only the sound of their own footsteps. In the dressing room, it hit them that they needed an instant song that the hordes would readily get up and dance to. A Paul Rodgers interview some years later contradicted this to some extent. As he pointed out, they'd had the sure-fire crowd-pleasing last song in their set for most of their history: namely 'The Hunter'.

What is beyond doubt is they needed another number with that same instantly infectious spirit, and preferably one they'd written themselves. One of the prerequisites was to have a really catchy memorable chorus, and either Paul or Andy, not surprisingly, started singing 'All right now, baby it's all right now'. A couple of chords were added and the song grew from that, with Paul supplying the narrative beginning with a girl being eyed up in the street. The musical inspiration could've come from any number of sources – not least the Stones' 'Jumpin' Jack Flash' with its 'But it's all right now' chorus phrase, or the feel of 'Honky Tonk Women', with its basic chord foundation. Instinctively, they knew they had a winner. At one gig, they played it at the start almost without rehearsing. Towards the end of the show, Paul asked the audience if there were any requests during the short time left, or did they want them to play anything again. Almost as one, the audience called out for another performance of 'that first one you did'. That, they knew, was enough to confirm that the song was making an immediate impact.

Later in January, they returned to Morgan Studios to begin work on album three. Neither Guy Stevens nor Chris Blackwell were around, and an overworked Andy Johns was present when they arrived at the studio with their gear. He told his assistant he'd been working very long days non-stop for several months and needed a rest, so he left them to it. As he pretended not to be there, they spent a few hours playing and trying things with the assistant, before leaving. Their next destination was Trident Studios with the young new engineer Roy Thomas Baker. This would be their home from home for the next two months until the second week in March. Whenever they had a break in their touring schedule, they returned there to record, eventually putting down seven new numbers. 'Don't Say You Love Me' would long be associated with an amusing memory. It was a song Paul and Andy had written late at night at the latter's house in Roehampton when they were both quite tired, hence the relaxed mood. Not long afterwards, they were playing Newcastle City Hall when the chief of police arrived, either having had reports of impending trouble, or expecting something of the kind to erupt. He walked on to the front of the stage with his back to the band, arms folded and looked threateningly at the audience. Paul Rodgers stopped the band and told them to play the song – really gently. The audience were pacified immediately and fell quiet. Exit one rather embarrassed senior police officer without a word (having realised that everything was all right now, one might say), to the amusement of musicians and punters alike.

After two months of recording on and off, the band had completed the album with assistance from Roy Baker, and delivered the masters to Island, convinced they now knew enough to be able to do everything themselves. When Chris Blackwell listened to the result, he called a meeting at the office and told them it would never do, as it was unfinished; it sounded too live, too sparse, required overdubs, and above all, needed remixing. He was sure 'All Right Now' had major hit potential once some work was done, but at over six minutes it was much too long for a single and would never get played on the radio. Would they cut it down, remove or at least compact the guitar solo and take a verse out as well? Although they kept quiet about it, they'd recorded the song three times, the first attempt being a rather more poppy version a little over three minutes long with an a cappella chorus as intro, backing vocals, maracas and tambourines but no guitar solo; to say nothing of Simon and Andy getting down on their knees and hammering the Hammond organ bass pedals with their fists.

This was one battle they knew they couldn't win. They left the offices thoroughly deflated. But a few successful gigs raised their spirits again, and after another BBC session in April, they reluctantly returned to the studio. Chris Blackwell had chosen John Kelly to co-produce the album, insisting that the band overdub the original masters and then remix everything. It was something of a compromise, with neither Blackwell (who was effectively co-producer with Kelly, though uncredited on the cover) nor the band completely happy with the result. He had stood firm on editing 'All Right Now' for the single, taking out the first section of the guitar solo and the final verse: or rather, the third verse (which was in fact the second one repeated after the guitar break), but allowed the full 5½-minute album version to remain intact. The editing reduced the single to a more compact 4¼ minutes, in order not to jeopardise their chances of airplay.

'All Right Now' was released as a single in May, with 'Mouthful Of Grass' on the B-side. It coincided with the group's appearance at the Hollywood Festival, Newcastle-under-Lyme, on the weekend of 23/24 May, headlined by Grateful Dead, with Traffic, Black Sabbath, José Feliciano and the previously almost unknown Mungo Jerry, who ended up stealing the show. After playing on the Sunday afternoon, Free were called back for two encores. The media reaction was immediate, with one prominent exception being the opinion of Roger Daltrey when he was played the record in *Melody Maker*'s Blind Date session. He conceded, 'Good voice, though the tune is a bit meaningless,' but that it must be a B-side, as he could not imagine anyone releasing it as an A-side, and thought it must be Fleetwood Mac. 'Oh dear, I'm really not interested and I don't care!'

Fortunately for Free, almost everyone else *did* care. Music journalists leapt on it immediately, full of praise, and in its first week it entered the charts at number 36. Fortuitously, The Rolling Stones were in the process of changing record companies and launching their own label, and a gap of almost two years without a new single from them worked very much to Free's advantage. The music weeklies all heralded them as the group to replace The Stones; even calling them 'the new Stones', and some journalists immediately made comparisons between Mick Jagger's stage presence and Paul's fronting of the band with the mic stand as a prop if not a weapon. Suddenly hot property, Free's booking fee rocketed to twice what it had been at the beginning of the summer, if not more.

A mixed blessing came in the shape of a request from the BBC for Free to appear on *Top Of The Pops* that week. None of them had any great desire to appear on the show that could immediately send a new release sky-high. But despite having made strenuous efforts in the previous few months to include rock and progressive acts with the pop groups and middle-of-the-road entertainers, some still saw *Top Of The Pops* as a kids' show that could destroy a band's credibility at once. Nevertheless, the band's management – hell-bent on a hit for their brightest hope – insisted it would be good for business. The TV production team had to check the lyrics carefully, listening several times to satisfy themselves that Paul was singing 'Let's move before they raise the parking rate' at the end of the first verse, and not 'the fucking rent'. (As the line had to rhyme with 'don't hesitate', to anybody listening properly, it must've been obvious.) Having passed the profanity test and spent a tedious few hours rehearsing and perfecting camera angles, the group were allowed on. Paul insisted on being allowed to sing live to their backing track – something other bands were increasingly doing – the other three miming their instruments with ill-concealed disdain in front of the cameras. At least they could bask in the knowledge that they'd hit the big time when Island sent a car around to drive them to the TV studio.

As far as Island were concerned, the sacrifice paid off. A meteoric rise in the singles chart from number 27 to number four in one week, culminating in five weeks at number two (unable to dislodge fellow Hollywood Festival heroes Mungo Jerry's 'In The Summertime') cemented 'All Right Now' as one of the major hits of the year. Its success spread across the Atlantic, and by October, a slow but measured rise in sales propelled it to number four in the *Billboard* chart. In Britain, it became Island's fastest-selling record ever, and at one point was flying out of the shops at an estimated rate of 1,000 copies an hour. Pressing plants could barely keep up with the demand, amid rumours that a few more supplies in the shops would've sent it to number one in the official UK chart, as it was for two or three weeks in the weekly music papers. Free blazed a trail for others to follow. In the remaining six months of 1970, Deep Purple, Black Sabbath and Jimi Hendrix likewise had their highest-ever charting British singles.

Andy conceded that the record was indeed the hit they'd so eagerly sought, but it was a two-edged sword: 'You end up questioning your integrity: standing, miming on *Top of the Pops*. Our fan base were male blues fans, and when all the girls started nudging their way into the gigs, the guys got a little peeved. They thought we'd sold out.' Koss broadly agreed, stressing that 'All Right Now' was not the song they wanted to be remembered for, although it had benefited them in that it brought a whole new audience along to gigs.

Only after the single was climbing the top 40 did the album sessions come to an end: much to the relief of John Kelly. It had initially been scheduled for release in July. After another programme of mixing and overdubbing, all remaining work had to be expedited when it was given priority for issue in the last week of June, as advance orders boosted by sales of the single had reached the 30,000 mark.

Free: Fire And Water *(1970)*

Personnel:
Paul Rodgers: vocals
Paul Kossoff: guitar
Andy Fraser: bass, piano, acoustic guitar
Simon Kirke: drums, percussion, acoustic guitar
Producers: Free, John Kelly
Engineer: Roy Baker
Recorded at Island Studios and Trident Studios, London, January–June 1970
Release date: 26 June 1970
Chart placings: UK: 2, US: 17
Running time: 35:01
All songs by Rodgers/Fraser unless stated otherwise
Side One: 1. Fire And Water 2. Oh I Wept (Rodgers, Kossoff) 3. Remember 4. Heavy Load
Side Two: 1. Mr Big (Rodgers, Fraser, Kossoff, Kirke) 2. Don't Say You Love Me 3. All Right Now
Bonus tracks on subsequent CD reissues: Oh I Wept (Alternate vocal), Fire And Water (Stereo mix), Fire And Water (BBC session), All Right Now (BBC session), All Right Now (Single edit), All Right Now (Early version)

Of all the tracks Free never released as singles, the title track probably heads the list as the best. It's also the shortest song here, being the only one under four minutes long. It's built around a basic but easily memorable and quite catchy guitar riff, a dazzling lead break, and is supported well by bass and piano, and even the makings of a brief drum solo as it fades: something that could perhaps have been developed a little more. As for the vocal, it must go down as one of Paul Rodgers' strongest performances from this era. Talking to Roy Carr of *NME* shortly after the album was released, Paul said the song had been in his mind for several months when they toured America with Blind Faith. He was impressed with and influenced by what he called the 'whole new soul sound emerging in the States', as exemplified by James Brown and Sly and the Family Stone, which to him sounded much stronger and cleaner than before, with 'a genuine and sincere feeling for the music'. He was thrilled when Wilson Pickett recorded his own version of 'Fire And Water' the following year, and it reached the US Billboard top 30. Paul said a cover had partly been his intention, as with his love of the genre, he really wanted to write a song that one of the soul greats could do with ease: 'I didn't think they actually would! In those days, I held them as if they lived in paradise, and I would never get to be in touch with them.' Pickett's version – a slightly faster rendition with brass, backing vocals and swinging tambourine – was certainly much more tailor-made for the dance floor than the original.

'Oh I Wept' is a more downbeat, relaxed song, with the rhythm section supporting the vocals, and, as ever, Paul Kossoff's restrained, charmingly minimalist guitar solo with that expressive tremolo soaring up and down the scale. For most of the song, he is adding the lightest touch on his instrument, above a steady but unobtrusive rhythm section. Paul Rodgers' relaxed vocal is tinged with sadness but looks to a better future as he sings of taking his seat on the train and letting the sun melt away his pain, as he will soon bask in the sunshine of another day. He admitted it was a case of writing about his personal experiences. But as the writing credits suggest, it was more the guitarist's song than Paul's.

'Remember' follows a similar path – the lyrics reminiscing about summer days and wandering around in the northern heat, Paul Rodgers being the only northerner making that rather a giveaway. There's a pungent little lead guitar intro and lead break, plus muscular rhythm guitar throughout, hand in glove with the bass and drums, while the occasional piano chord or two provide good support. The piano dominates the backing throughout, with another of Paul Kossoff's sparing and wonderfully concise guitar solos about halfway through.

Simple piano, like the start of an old classical piece, introduces 'Heavy Load' – possibly a metaphor for life in its lyrics about carrying a heavy load down a long road. It was created more or less spontaneously in the studio, and Paul Rodgers remarked afterwards that it was his favourite on the album.

'Mr. Big' – the song that gave a 1990s American band their name (and perhaps the late 1970s British band too), is a slow but menacing number. Is Paul singing to a love rival, telling Mr. Big to 'Get out of here before I lose my cool'? His restrained howl of anger brings the song to a crescendo in the last few seconds. When asked about the song, he said it was inspired by B.B. King and 'his approach to womanhood'. It was one of their most popular live numbers, and though it began life as Paul's song, he agreed to a four-way writing credit, as they all put a great deal into its creation. Andy's bass solo is probably the finest he ever did, edging its way around the fretboard, while Paul Kossoff's muffled power chords hover in the background.

After almost six minutes of carefully controlled aggression comes six minutes of ballad: the longest song on the album. 'Don't Say You Love Me' is the one that had notably defused a potentially difficult situation onstage, as related above. One wonders if Paul Rodgers again had in mind a soul singer – the likes of Al Green or Timmy Thomas – to cover this. The guitar, piano, bass and drums here are all a masterclass in control and holding back – until close to the end when they all move up a notch, Kossoff adds a solo and Simon Kirke goes into action on the cymbals.

So, no blues in evidence, and nothing approaching fast hard rock to be heard – until 'All Right Now': the song that opened the whole world up for them. Its contrast with the rest of the album is remarkable. About three quarters of nearly any Rolling Stones album would have the average partygoer out on the dance floor. But the band whom some now called 'the new Stones' handled things differently. Anyone reading this will know the single version inside out, but after having been so used to Blackwell's grimly necessary radio edit, will welcome the chance to appreciate the full five minutes plus workout and the two-part guitar solo if they haven't heard it already.

Over the years, 'All Right Now' attracted several cover versions. In 1975, it was Ohio R&B singer Lea Roberts' (whose voice was sometimes likened to Aretha Franklin's) only British release (with a little obvious lyric gender-tweaking), and was played several times on Capital Radio, but without any chart action. In 1979, disco group Witch Queen issued a cover in Canada only, and Rod Stewart made a very 1980s electropop single in 1984 that became a minor American hit. Later, Pepsi & Shirlie also recorded it, as did Christina Aguilera. Paul Rodgers praised the latter as 'absolutely rocking... it's quite hard to pull off, really, but she gave it some stick'.

The first two albums had gone for a rather arty cover design approach. This time, the group name, album title and a large photo of all four seated together without any background distractions, earnestly facing the viewer, burned their way instantly into the public eye. This was evidently no smiling, jolly pop group, but a statement from a mean and moody quartet who meant business with no frills.

Paul Rodgers admitted that they enjoyed making this album far more than the first two. As comparative newcomers, they were 'very nervous' with the first and dissatisfied with the result, while the second was much too clean. This time they were pleased with the feel and the sound they achieved. It remained fairly sparse, uncluttered – evidently a little too much so for Chris Blackwell's liking, whose production on the second record had not satisfied the band. *Fire And Water* had taken up much more studio time than the others, but in their view, it was justified by the results. Koss was of similar mind, saying that the first two had been 'more or less stepping stones'; the first album had been 'very rough', and the second 'too crisp and clean'. They were much happier with the third, which was 'pretty close to what we are all about now'.

As for the criticism that they had 'sold out' to the teen audience, they insisted that nothing could be further from the truth. It was evident that just one single had put them firmly on the map, brought them far more live work, and also helped to provide them with an equally successful album. The downside was the younger age of some of the audiences, especially screaming young girls, whose unrestrained behaviour wherever they played began to evoke comparisons with Beatlemania.

Unfortunately, the lack of a Beatle haircut proved to be the vocalist's undoing on one occasion. When Paul Rodgers and *Melody Maker* staff writer Chris Charlesworth went to unwind at a club one night, the doorman wouldn't let Paul in because his hair was too long, even though their copy of 'All Right Now' was on the deck, blaring loud and clear from speakers at the edge of the dance floor. He promptly demanded that their copy of the single be handed over to them, and they returned to their hotel.

So where did Free fit on the musical spectrum? They never claimed to be heavy rock, or even progressive, but were basically blues and soul: the genres that had always inspired them most of all. Speaking to Jerry Floyd of *ZigZag* in August, Koss emphasised that soul music was what they were all into most of all, and it was bound to influence them. They played songs, 'rather than long pieces with complicated time changes and rhythm patterns'. He accepted that such a principle was valid for some bands, but it was not for them, and he did not think their audiences would find that approach acceptable. 'They want something that's easily understood, easy to grasp.' Their objective was to go out and play to people, make records and have a good time. 'We'd rather enjoy ourselves than come out with all this serious stuff about messages, or trying to play anything startlingly new.'

In July 1970, Free toured Germany and the Netherlands on an Island Records package with Traffic (who had recently reformed and were headlining) and Bronco. The members of all three bands bonded well, with Traffic drummer Jim Capaldi becoming a firm friend, and Free sharing their equipment with Bronco each night. On their return, they played several more British dates. At a service station where they stopped to refuel their Transit van, a small, slightly balding man with glasses and a college scarf came up to tell them what a fantastic record they had out. The only one who recognised him as Elton John was Andy, as he'd bought Elton's last album.

With a single and album both riding high in the charts, Island were anxious for the follow-up. One album every few months, recorded as quickly and cheaply as possible, was the norm to keep the momentum going and the cash coming in. On 18 August, they went into Island Studios for a week, then spent the last weekend at the Isle of Wight, where they played the Bank Holiday festival for the second year running – on a bill that included Jimi Hendrix making what would be his last major appearance in Britain, The Who, Joni Mitchell, Joan Baez, Jethro Tull, Chicago, and – on their festival debut – the newly launched Emerson, Lake & Palmer. A year before, when they first played the festival, Free had been relative unknowns, but now they were anything but. As they were about to cross over on the mainland ferry, Pete Townshend recognised them in the car, tapped on their window and told them that the current hit was the best record he'd heard all year.

But delays and technical problems meant that the festival's running schedule was disrupted, and what was to have been a Saturday night slot was postponed until Sunday morning. Several thousand festivalgoers emerged bleary-eyed from their sleeping bags, yet were soon up on their feet to a set that included three songs from the forthcoming album, alongside 'Fire And Water', 'Mr. Big', 'I'm A Mover' and the last three inevitably being 'The Hunter', 'All Right Now' and 'Crossroads'.

For much of September, October and into the first week of November, gigs were interspersed with several days of studio time. The two gigs that would be best remembered were a couple of shows on the same night – one at 6:00 p.m. and one at 8:45 p.m. at Fairfield Halls, Croydon, both with Mott The Hoople as support. Having a few live recordings in the can from early in the year at Sunderland – and perhaps having been inspired by the recent successes of the Stones' *Get Yer Ya-Ya's Out!* and The Who's *Live at Leeds* – Island decided this gig would be a good opportunity to add to the collection, for release whenever the time was right. Andy Johns accordingly took the Pye mobile equipment along to the venue to capture it for posterity.

The next album marked a change of approach, for the songs they recorded on the first three albums had been written, rehearsed, tried and tested while they were on the road. With pressure from Chris Blackwell to release a fourth album quickly – and with only around three songs already completed and tried out onstage so far – they had to write some of the others in the studio. In spite of this, they found it the easiest of the four albums to record, with none of the disagreements between band, producers and management that had threatened to overshadow the others.

Once again, there was a marked musical change. One record of almost pure blues, one more folky and acoustic, and one much rockier, was followed by one that suggested a more Dylanesque / country rock / Southern boogie influence. During their last few listening sessions, Otis Redding's *Otis Blue*, Elton John's *Tumbleweed Connection*, and above all The Band's *Music From Big Pink,* had all featured strongly. Andy Fraser's piano and keyboards were becoming ever-more prominent, and as he and Paul Rodgers were still writing the majority of the material, it was a change the other two were none too pleased about. Simon accepted the situation with apathy, and Koss was feeling increasingly out on a limb, with the band moving further away from their roots and finding more solace in drink and drugs. Moreover, the sudden 18 September death of Jimi Hendrix – whom Koss had always deeply revered – affected him far more deeply than the others.

Free: Highway *(1970)*

Personnel:

Paul Rodgers: vocals

Paul Kossoff: guitar

Andy Fraser: bass, piano, keyboards, acoustic guitar

Simon Kirke: drums, percussion
Producer: Free
Engineer: Andy Johns
Recorded at Island Studios, London, August–November 1970
Release date: December 1970
Chart placings: UK: 41, US: 190
Running time: 35:58
All songs by Rodgers/Fraser unless stated otherwise
Side One: 1. The Highway Song (Fraser, Kossoff) 2. The Stealer (Rodgers, Fraser, Kossoff) 3. On My Way 4. Be My Friend
Side Two: 1. Sunny Day (Rodgers, Fraser, Kossoff, Kirke) 2. Ride On Pony 3. Love You So (Rodgers, Kirke) 4. Bodie 5. Soon I Will Be Gone
Bonus tracks on 2002 CD reissue: My Brother Jake, Only My Soul, Ride On A Pony (BBC session), Be My Friend (BBC session), Rain (Alternate version), The Stealer (Single version)

Free's almost-country-rock album begins with 'The Highway Song'. A relaxed tune led by piano and drums, it aims at something of a story in the lyrics, albeit an incomplete one. They will make you smile. Our narrator – who may be one of a team – was working in the cornfield, but got distracted, so he or they never brought the bucket back. The farmer had a daughter who was evidently a little on the flighty side, so he went to get his gun, whereupon our hero explains they were just having drunken fun. She never spoke a word, but later they were overheard kissing her in the orchard (ah, a third person is involved) – and that's where it ends. This was the song they said was most inspired by The Band, and it's probably closer to pop than anything on the earlier albums, with a memorable tune and a catchy element that would perhaps have lent itself to a cover version or two.

With pressure on to record not just another album but also another sure-fire hit song, 'The Stealer' was planned as the one. Recorded at the end of August, it has the same kind of raw grit as 'All Right Now' – if not such an instant hook – and a good guitar solo that was surprisingly edited from not only the single but also the album version. However, the band were thrilled with the results and could not wait to share them. After the first take – at about 3:00 in the morning – Andy Johns went to Chris Blackwell's flat, banged on his door and urged him to come down to the studio and listen to it, because it was going to be another massive single. Despite being roused at such an unearthly hour, he readily agreed, if only to be allowed to get back to bed quickly afterwards. The engineer was very impressed at being able to approach the owner of the record company in such a way: 'You can't do that with Ahmet Ertegun!' (head of Atlantic Records).

'On My Way' is more mellow, with vague suggestions of romance in the lyrics. Paul Kossoff's guitar is confined largely to rhythm, and the main musical element is Andy's keyboard work sounding like a harmonium, supported by a shuffle on the drums.

At almost six minutes, 'Be My Friend' is the album's longest track, and rather outstays its welcome. A ballad with simple lyrics appealing for love and friendship, it builds gently from Andy's opening on the piano, with Mellotron coming in later, and another very precise and quite sparing guitar break towards the end. In its basic tenderness, it shares some common ground with a number of songs on George Harrison's *All Things Must Pass*, released at around the same time. But whereas the co-producer of the latter – Phil Spector – wrapped those songs in a lavish wall of sound, the relatively stark instrumentation that Free used never really seems enough, especially with a song of this length and a repetitive lyric that towards the end could have given way rather earlier to a lead break. The band all loved it, and when they were previewing the finished album for the music press, Andy told Roy Carr of *NME* – an avid supporter of the band at the time – that it was their personal favourite; Paul Rodgers even saying he thought it was the best thing they had ever done.

Much the same can be said for side two's opener 'Sunny Day', which Andy called 'nothing more than a little buzz… just like one basic idea'. It's another low-key adventure, with a lyric that sings of a sunny day melting away, while a spurned lover dwells on the end of his affair, having been a fool and given his woman everything, when all she did was lie to him. There are elements of a tune here, but it's all too restrained, and the feeling that it might develop into something more substantial towards the end – over and above the guitar, piano and bass – are never realised.

'Ride On Pony' (sometimes given as 'Ride (or Riding) On A Pony' or 'Ride A Pony') – the song that Blackwell preferred as a single when he heard the full album – is closer to the Free that fans were probably expecting. Paul Rodgers' soulful vocal sounds more heartfelt as they weave around a muscular riff, culminating in what's probably Koss' best solo on the album: which competes with the vocal for centre stage towards the end, as the drums also build in intensity.

'Love You So' – the first Rodgers/Kirke composition to make it to a Free album, apparently written in the back of the van while on their way to a gig one night is – as the title suggests – another charming, pretty love song, with equally charming piano and guitar. Paul's intense vocals towards the end are matched by additional fire on the drums.

Another story-song of sorts, 'Bodie' tells of a boy who comes from the country hills to see the world, and finds himself a town girl who 'showed him the good life and made herself his wife'. This is rather like a reversion to the folksiness of some of the songs on the second album, with Andy's acoustic guitar providing most of the flavour and just the hint of a country twang from Koss.

Paul Rodgers picks up an acoustic guitar himself for the first time on the closing track 'Soon I Will Be Gone', while Andy adds piano and Mellotron, and a gentle tambourine comes in later. A gentle swaying song, rather like a waltz, tells of a love affair gone wrong, and the narrator will not forget her, but he is leaving. However, just when a big finish sounds as if it might be in order, it comes to a rather sudden end. Many years later, Paul said it was the song that he was most proud of having written: 'I like the chord structure and I like the sadness of it. Any song is about the mood; you're capturing the mood you're in, and you're recreating that every time you play it.'

Following two fairly arty album cover designs, followed by a third that showed band, album and title unmistakably on the front, Island went even further along the bold, innovative road this time, but they overstepped the boundary of common sense. The cover showed four heads in adjacent vertical columns, looking like screen prints in pale beige with pale blue backgrounds: a rather unappealing combination. Close inspection of the basic portrait of each member reveals one letter from the band name superimposed several hundred times, with the album title helpfully printed larger on the top. The band were not consulted and were distinctly unimpressed with the result. Andy Johns was so furious that he demanded a meeting with Blackwell to ask him, 'Who the fuck is responsible for this piece of shit?' Blackwell owned up that it was him. Overseas pressings had the good sense to add the band name in much larger letters. But having an album in the stores where would-be buyers had to look at the back to satisfy themselves who the artist really was did it no favours. One paper reviewed the album in all good faith, saying, 'This new band Highway sound like Free.' Another wrote a short piece praising the new release from Highway, who had 'a touch of the Rolling Stones' influence', mentioning the Island catalogue number but with no reference to Free. Once the error was pointed out, they printed an apology a week later.

Despite Island wanting 'Ride On Pony' as the new single, the band stuck to their guns. 'The Stealer' (or just 'Stealer' according to the label of the British release) was released at the end of October. *Melody Maker* called it 'an abject lesson in how to make hit records: simple, heavy, moody but believable'. *NME* rated it 'as close to a chart certainty as you could ever get', and predicted that it would 'soon be up there challenging for number 1'. In a month that saw the Jimi Hendrix Experience single 'Voodoo Chile' top the British charts for one week, anything was possible. Yet despite everyone's expectations, 'The Stealer' only reached number 49 in America and stalled completely at home, with the scant consolation of being top 20 in Austria and top 40 in Germany.

After what had virtually amounted to a recurrence of Beatlemania in the summer – with reports in the press of security staff having to hold screaming fans back and stop them from trying to tear out locks of their heroes' hair as souvenirs – they might have been content to shrug off a single that flopped. Andy told *Mirabelle* magazine's Chris Kendrick: 'Thankfully, as a band, we are not existing on the strength of our last single.' It was just as well, for after the meteoric success of 'All Right Now', hardly anybody expected 'The Stealer' to miss the top 20, let alone the top 50 altogether. So when it did, the shock was palpable. Airplay on Radio 1 was as minimal as press advertising, and despite glowing reviews, maybe people simply did not know the single was out.

The album followed in December, with the music weeklies generally giving it a good deal of praise. Ray Telford in *Sounds* said it was 'definitely one of the best albums of the year'. Yet hot on the heels of a flop single, it fared little better, spending two weeks in the lower reaches of the top 50 in January. A national postal strike that resulted in the album chart being truncated to a top 30 (even sometimes a top 29) after those two weeks and continuing thus until the end of March, may have denied it a few weeks of further glory. Nevertheless, a single that had caught fire like a rocket and taken an album with it had been followed by a failed single and a scarcely more successful long player. Like it or not, a major hit was the key to everything, with Led Zeppelin being the exception to the rule.

So why was *Highway* such a commercial failure? The media evidently enjoyed it, though retrospective opinion is divided. Some fans were impressed that the band were not repeating themselves by issuing what could've amounted to a son of *Fire And Water*, while others thought that much of *Highway* was insipid and an ill-advised stab at country rock by a group who were not cut out for such a style and should've stuck to what they did best. Releasing an album so close to Christmas was often considered risky, with even sure-fire massive sellers by the top names generally held over until early new year for maximum impact. In hindsight, the most likely explanation was that Island were killing the goose that laid the golden egg, and perhaps with a record that was – all things considered – a little too pop or easy listening for its target audience. There is some justification for saying that some of the songs – perhaps too many – were straying an unexpectedly long way from blues and rock. A few more weeks, even a few more months, would've given them time to recharge their batteries and come roaring back with the ultimate Free album for the spring of 1971.

The album's failure hit all four of them hard, and perhaps Koss the hardest of all. At around the time it was released, there were suggestions that an as yet little known but soon to be huge collaborator was ready to work with him. Rod Stewart – who joined The Faces earlier that year as vocalist (following the exit of Steve Marriott from what had been Small Faces) and had also just released two solo albums with another label – gave an interview in the music press saying he was really knocked out by the music of Free. He was planning to write some songs with Paul Kossoff for his next solo album, as the latter was brimming over with ideas that never got a chance because Rodgers and Fraser had such a virtual monopoly on new Free songs. Rod repeated the idea several months later when approached by another publication, as he was about to record his third solo album, which would make him a huge star (again, thanks to a massive hit single, a transatlantic number one). For Koss, it could've all turned out so differently (a Back Street Crawler collaboration with Rod the Mod?) had he not been increasingly in thrall to the demons that would cut both his career and life so tragically short.

Chapter Three: 1971

In January 1971, Free embarked on a coast-to-coast tour of America. For them, it was a pleasant change to be accepted properly by their audiences, without the screaming crowds that had greeted them in England during the last few months. Here the shows were more sedate, with everyone receptive to the more laid-back *Highway* material. Andy was playing piano onstage much more, especially on songs from the new album, and another he'd just written (although it was credited as ever to Rodgers/ Fraser): the as yet unrecorded 'My Brother Jake'. Most of the shows proved to be very successful, though after three years of constant touring, band relationships were beginning to come under strain. As the dates drew to a close at the end of January, Blackwell decided that in order to consolidate their status in America, it would be important to bring them back before long. Plans were made for them to return in May with a larger itinerary, this time with Mott The Hoople as support.

Returning to Britain, in February, they embarked on another trek around the nation, with fellow Island band Amazing Blondel. After a show at the Civic Hall, Guildford, they went out to one of the local pubs, leaving their van fully packed with gear behind the venue. Coming back a few hours later, they found all their equipment had been stolen and had to hire everything they needed in a hurry for the next few dates. After that, it was some compensation the following month when they were told they'd broken the house attendance record (previously held by The Rolling Stones) at the Lyceum Ballroom in London. In spite of the failure of their last album and single, they were still one of the most popular concert acts in the country.

Everyone was convinced that they had to draw a line under what might prove to be no more than a brief setback. A few days of studio sessions in March yielded several new tracks – among them 'My Brother Jake': a jaunty, even slightly singalong number with piano and Mellotron. Andy Fraser said it was written about his friend Jamaican singer Horace Faith, but 'brother Jake' sounded better than 'brother Horace'. What problems the latter had that Andy should advise him to start again and make some friends, or what had gone wrong with him and why his candle was burning, was never explained. Andy Johns admitted he didn't like the song much and probably foresaw that as a lightweight pop number, it would cut little ice with fans, but he could see it had the charm that might attract teen buyers. Island desperately wanted a second hit single to compensate for the under-achieving 'The Stealer' on which they had staked so much. Another new number from the same sessions – 'Only My Soul' – was the B-side, and the resulting release hit the shops in April. To general relief, it appealed to buyers in their thousands, and within a month it peaked at number four for two weeks, although it failed in America. The *NME* chart placed it at number one, thus giving Free two chart-toppers: either side of a complete stiff.

But it came too late to save Free from self-destructing. Fraser/Rodgers had indeed been the new Lennon/McCartney in a sense; the ever more prolific and increasingly eclectic songwriters who'd come up with enough new songs for a major share of four albums within three years. By the beginning of 1971, they were increasingly writing on their own. It didn't make any real difference to the songwriting credits. Sometime earlier, Alexis Korner had suggested to Andy – who discussed it with Paul Rodgers – that since they were writing combinations of everything together, it would make sense to split the credits equally. Andy conceded that Paul was writing more, but as bass guitarist and keyboard player, Andy was putting much more into arrangements, 'and it's going to pan out eventually'. Rarely did Andy also write the lyrics – except in the case of 'My Brother Jake' which was entirely his work – or Paul the music. Splitting their efforts down the middle simplified the whole process.

However, by now, the relationship was crumbling, as the other two looked on with increasing dismay. According to the easygoing Simon, Paul Rodgers was undeniably the best singer around, and as a person, was very intense, charming and with a great sense of humour on a good day, but moody and even belligerent at other times. Andy was a musical prodigy and multi-instrumentalist with a first-class business brain, but was too much of a know-all, showing the others exactly how guitar or drums were to be played on a particular track. Andy Johns praised him for his great arrangements, while not forgetting to credit Simon for his often-overlooked acoustic guitar and backing vocal skills, or Koss for his fantastic guitar sound. Richard Digby-Smith – who was now regularly assisting as an engineer, tape operator and mixer – was likewise impressed with the talent and creativity he saw being unleashed – the way Paul Rodgers would put his vocals on tape, and Koss then overdub his guitar around them, whereas most other groups would do the opposite. Yet Digby-Smith also saw the frustration, aggression and short fuses between them. While Paul's musical skills steadily improved, as did Andy's lyrical prowess, they both became more confident and self-assertive – insisting that songs had to be done their way – and less inclined to compromise.

Koss – who had regarded Free as his life for the last three years – told them he thought the situation was ridiculous, and instead of making a big scene, said, 'Let's just go in the studio and do it.' Simon, the eldest, said that splitting up was the worst thing they could've done: caused by 'a lot of silly bickering'. All they really needed was a good manager or another Alexis Korner-like father figure to tell them to go and take a year off, not a record label and management keeping them on the hamster wheel, demanding more and more made-to-order product for the money machine. Paul felt that Andy's stranglehold on everything to do with the band and its music was tightening, and he wanted out.

They decided to keep the decision to themselves for the time being, agreeing that it should be business as usual – giving press interviews, recording BBC and TV sessions as required, in addition to honouring Japanese and Australian dates to which they were already committed. Only when sitting next to horrified tour manager Johnny Glover on the plane to Japan did Andy reveal that this was to be the end for them. The previous evening, he and Paul Rodgers had jointly told Chris Blackwell they were going to break up the band once the tour was over.

They played two shows in Japan – one at Kanda and one at Tokyo, the second ending in a crowd riot that was only quelled when the band were brought back onstage at the end of the show for three more numbers. By the time they reached Australia for the remaining four dates, the tension offstage was becoming even worse, with Paul Rodgers and Andy almost coming to physical blows. At the end of the show on 9 May at Randwick Racecourse, Sydney, Paul symbolically flung his mic stand into the wings as a final gesture that their last gig was over. Planning had already begun for the American tour, and Glover was tasked with having to stop everything in its tracks before any dates were scheduled.

A thoroughly displeased Island management team accordingly began a damage limitation exercise. Statements were issued to the music press saying it had been an amicable split, the four members having achieved as much as they could within the group.

Three new outfits were to emerge from the old one, and a new live album was released the following month. The tapes that had been made at the Sunderland and Croydon shows the year before would be put to good use. It was almost as if somebody at Island, looking at their volatile 'new Stones', had seen the split coming.

Free: Free Live! (1971)

Personnel:
Paul Rodgers: vocals
Paul Kossoff: guitar
Andy Fraser: bass, piano, acoustic guitar
Simon Kirke: drums
Recorded live at Fillmore Ballroom, Fillmore North, The Locarno, Sunderland, January 1970 (Tracks 1, 7); Fairfield Halls, Croydon, September 1970 (2–6); 'Get Where I Belong' recorded at Island Studios, March 1971, produced by Andy Johns.
Release date: June 1971
Chart placings: UK: 4, US: 89
Running time: 40:33
All songs by Rodgers/Fraser unless stated otherwise
Side One: 1. All Right Now 2. I'm A Mover 3. Be My Friend 4. Fire And Water
Side Two: 1. Ride On A Pony 2. Mr. Big 3. The Hunter (Booker T. Jones, Carl Wells, Donald Dunn, Al Jackson Jr., Steve Cropper) 4. Get Where I Belong
Bonus tracks on 2002 CD reissue: Woman, Walk In My Shadow, Moonshine, Trouble On Double Time, Mr. Big (Alternative take), All Right Now (Alternative take), Get Where I Belong (Alternative take)

That the song generally kept for near the end of the show on a live (or seven-eighths live) album was placed first, suggests that marketing decisions (undoubtedly Blackwell's) took priority over any attempt at a realistic running order. It undoubtedly sets the scene well, with the crowd going wild as the drum intro begins. As this version of the newly written 'All Right Now' was recorded before they attempted it in the studio, they were evidently still fine-tuning it. The lead break pattern follows a similar path to that of the full album version, except for the guitar solo coming in a little later, with the three musicians carrying on for nearly a minute after the chorus is over. The general recording has a few rough edges, but as Paul explained to Roy Carr in another *NME* interview just before the album was released, there were mistakes on it that would not have been allowed to escape in the studio, yet he said the atmosphere on the Sunderland tracks was 'unbelievable'. The five Croydon tracks deviate little from the studio versions, though a burst of cheering as the crowd recognise 'Fire And Water' is noticeable. Likewise, when Paul exhorts the Sunderland punters to 'Sing it!' as they begin playing 'The Hunter', everyone goes wild again.

It cross-fades into 'Get Where I Belong', recorded at Island Studios during the spring sessions. At first, it sounds like a soothing love song, with much colour provided by Andy's electric piano and organ, plus a lead break that gives Koss free rein. However, when Koss spoke to Chris Charlesworth of *Melody Maker*, he said that they all 'feel very strongly about the studio track, which is a statement about what was happening within the group'.

Paul Rodgers told Roy Carr that he thought the live set was their best album to date. If only it was practically possible, he would like to record everything they ever released before an audience. Charlesworth seemed to agree, remarking in the review, 'Essentially a live group, it seems surprising that they have waited until they are no more before releasing a live album.' The sight of each individual member onstage, he continued, 'meant much more than the four studio albums that Island preciously presented us with'.

The album was packaged in a bootleg-style cover designed to look like an airmail envelope, with four postage stamp designs in the corner, each with the face of a band member, and an imitation postmark. At the time of release, interest in the band was at its height, in stark contrast to the poor sales reaction to *Highway* and 'The Stealer' at the beginning of the year. The live album subsequently spent 12 weeks in the chart, six of them in the top ten.

The three new bands that Island had promised were not long in materialising, and Glover was asked to take on the management of each. Paul Rodgers – who was more reluctant than the others to talk to the press about the break-up of Free, and was the most anxious to move on – formed a new trio, handling guitar duties as well as vocals, with Stewart McDonald from blues pub band Killing Floor on bass, and Mick Underwood from The Outlaws, The Herd and Episode Six on drums. Paul took the name Peace from a brand of Japanese cigarettes, and also as he 'wanted a bit of peace and to make music in a gentle manner and get away from the high pressure'.

Between September and December 1971, they played several dates, including a 14-city tour of England in October and November, again supporting Mott The Hoople. The bands bonded well, with Ian Hunter recommending to the rest of Mott that they should get Paul in on lead vocals so Ian could concentrate more on songwriting; Mick Ralphs also found much common ground with Paul on a personal and professional level. At a London Polytechnic gig without Mott, Koss joined Peace onstage for two encores, to an ecstatic reception.

During short breaks from touring, they booked some session time and completed six tracks. Of these, 'Lady' was released in 1974 on the first of several Free retrospectives: *The Free Story*, with 'Zero BC' and 'Like Water' appearing on *Songs of Yesterday* in 2000. Two more songs – 'Seven Angels' and 'Heartbreaker' – would be re-recorded by a reformed Free, and 'Do Right By Your Woman' and 'Like Water' later still by Bad Company. None of the songs were wasted. Paul also spent some time in Jamaica, where he recorded a reggae track with The Maytals: his song '(I Just Wanna) See You Smile'. It was produced by Chris Blackwell, with keyboard overdubs added in London a few weeks later by John 'Rabbit' Bundrick, a keyboard player who was working with Johnny Nash at the time and would soon join Free. Planned as a single in Jamaica only, no record of its release as such has been traced, and it was one of many rarities finally made available on *Songs of Yesterday*.

Andy formed the trio Toby, on vocals and bass, with guitarist Adrian Fisher and drummer Stan Speake. Between September and November, they recorded a 12-song demo, described by sources as 'uneven'. None of them were apparently released in any form, with only one song – 'Travellin' Man' – finding a new lease of life on what would be the next Free album. Three gigs supporting Amazing Blondel were scheduled for early November but cancelled.

Glover looked after both bands for about eight months. Afterwards, he said Peace was 'all right', but Toby was 'dreadful', while Paul remarked that Peace was 'a lot mellower' than Free.

Not to be outdone, Simon and Koss formed their own trio, working initially with bass guitarist Tetsu Yamauchi, whom they had befriended in Japan. Once it was evident that such a combination would not work, they connected with Rebop Kwaku Baah – a Ghanaian percussionist (discovered by Chris Blackwell) who joined Traffic when they reformed after a brief hiatus and also became – in effect – a resident session player for any other Island bands who needed one. He recommended they recruit Rabbit, who'd recently come to work in England. Koss and Simon were good team players, and Simon's skills as the diplomat and mediator went without saying. But having been part of a quartet in which the other two had always taken charge, the drummer and guitarist lacked musical leadership skills. Rabbit had several songs from demos he'd already sent to Blackwell, and these would form the bedrock of their sessions.

The ten-track album that gradually took shape included five of his songs, alongside two credited to Simon, a collaboration between Simon and Koss, an instrumental by Koss, plus a joint effort between Koss and Elliott Burgess. All four members shared vocals. As Koss was really missing Paul as a colleague, Simon phoned him to come along and listen in on rehearsals. When he did, he was impressed with what he heard, but said he was too preoccupied with getting Peace organised to contribute himself, and suggested they should find a new singer and go out on the road. As a result, once they'd recorded the backing tracks, they sorted out the vocals between them. Simon – who had evidently been hiding his light under a bushel for too long – agreed to step up to the mic on some and urged Rabbit to do likewise. The keyboard player's modest response was that he was playing with musicians who'd been used to sitting and playing with someone of Paul Rodgers' calibre, and he was a very hard act to follow. Encouraged by Simon, he agreed to 'have a go at it' on the grounds that if he gave it all he had, 'that's all you can do', and it would have more appeal than an album full of instrumentals.

Chapter Four: 1972

As promised, Island now had three bands instead of one. The two players who had been the driving force had each formed their own. But it would take the other two who – aided by a few other musicians – not only managed to enter the studio, but also emerged with an album in the shops to show for it within a few months.

Kossoff, Kirke, Tetsu, Rabbit: *Kossoff Kirke Tetsu Rabbit (1972)*

Personnel:
Paul Kossoff: guitar, vocals
John 'Rabbit' Bundrick: vocals, piano, electric piano, organ, Mellotron
Tetsu Yamauchi: bass
Simon Kirke: vocals, drums
Additional personnel:
B. J. Cole: steel guitar (Tracks 7, 9)
Producers: Kossoff, Kirke, Tetsu, Rabbit
Engineers: Richard Digby-Smith, Tony Platt
Recorded at Basing Street Studios, September–December 1971
Release date: April 1972
Chart placings: Did not chart
Running time: 43:57
Side One: 1. Blue Grass (Bundrick) 2. Sammy's Alright (Bundrick) 3. Anna (Kirke) 4. Just For The Box (Kossoff) 5. Hold On (Kirke, Kossoff)
Side Two: 1. Fool's Life (Bundrick) 2. Yellow House (Bundrick) 3. Dying Fire (Kirke) 4. I'm On The Run (Bundrick) 5. Colours (Elliott Burgess, Kossoff)

As the eponymous title implies, *Kossoff Kirke Tetsu Rabbit* amounts to a Free album without Rodgers and Fraser. It's hard to fault, at least on the grounds that it's all very well and tastefully played. Rabbit's keyboard skills are at least the equal of Andy Fraser's, and his work on the organ provides much of the colour, while B. J. Cole's pedal steel guitar adds to the palette on two tracks. Unfortunately, some of it lacks spirit, and at times the impression is of a band holding back and failing to catch fire. 'Hold On' – which seems to allude to the Free split with lines like 'When friends have turned to strangers' – reveals some passion. There is some spirit evident in 'I'm On The Run', and in 'Fool's Life', which hints vaguely at the tougher style Simon would adopt in the best of Bad Company's work later on. Another of his songs – 'Anna' – would also find a berth in the latter group. But the first version here – reliant on piano, organ and the rhythm section, without any guitar in earshot – only hints at what it would later become in different hands. The sole instrumental track 'Just For The Box' is credited to Koss as writer, and features what is probably his best work on the album: a wonderfully funky, slightly distorted, bone-crunching guitar sound.

Koss delivers some fine licks and an appealing solo on the opening track – Rabbit's 'Blue Grass' (maybe a pun on bluegrass, maybe not) – and on Simon's plaintive 'Dying Fire'. Koss also makes his vocal debut on 'Colours', which was in fact the only recording he ever made and released as a lead vocalist, but it had to be coaxed out of him with much persuasion from the others. Once everyone was ready for him to sing, he asked them to turn off the studio lights, as he wanted them to help create the proper atmosphere. They duly obliged, Digby rolled the tape, and they all waited for Koss to sing. When nothing happened, they turned the lights on again and saw he was fast asleep. They woke him up and he made his contribution, but very half-heartedly: and it shows. His guitar on this track is likewise a shadow of what it might once have been. On a good day (or evening), he proved that he could still really shine, but by this time his commitment to the music was evidently becoming all too erratic.

Rabbit makes a competent-enough singer, but Paul Rodgers was always going to be a hard act to follow. Contractual commitments may have prevented it, but one is tempted to wonder whether Rabbit ever thought of asking his friend and colleague Johnny Nash – who was enjoying a run of pop-reggae hits in Britain at the time – to come and help out as a guest vocalist.

Although his performances didn't always reach his best standards, Koss thoroughly enjoyed working with a full-time keyboard player: 'I realised at the time that working with keyboards – someone to take the middle register – it left me wide open to take a solo. Before, I was tending to fill the middle register, and when I'd take a solo, I'd come out of that and there was nothing to fill it, so there'd be a guitar up here and a bass way down there'.

Though he would be remembered more for his keyboard skills and session work with others, Rabbit emerges as a songwriter of no mean talent. 'Sammy's Alright' starts off with an attractive gospel-ish vocal, and the rest also has something of a spiritual feeling. His other outstanding contribution to the album – 'Yellow House' – combines country (due in part to B. J. Cole's wistful pedal steel) with an eastern flavour.

The album received mostly positive reviews, with Billy Walker of *Sounds* singling Kossoff out for praise: 'His playing shows a great deal of fluidity and touches of a more inventive progression'. Andrew Tyler of *Disc and Music Echo* noted in his review (three stars out of four), that 'the combination doesn't have the looseness of Free', and although Koss was a fine guitarist, his style became repetitious. To have allowed piano to take the lead more often, Tyler opined, would've helped improve the album. He singled out Kirke and Rabbit's harmonies as high points, proving that the absence of Paul Rodgers need not be universally regarded as a drawback. Nevertheless, the album never charted, and was probably seen by all but the most committed fans as just another one-off collaboration between star names and not-so-famous friends that was becoming all too commonplace in the early 1970s. An unimaginative front cover design – with the four names in brightly coloured bold uppercase against a light brown background – may not have helped sales.

By the time it slipped quietly into the shops, Free were back in business. Glover had foreseen that none of the three groups formed immediately after the split were really going to go far. Paul Rodgers and Andy both found that putting theirs together had been an expensive project that didn't look like paying dividends. Kossoff, Kirke, Tetsu and Rabbit were talking about taking their album out on tour, but none of them had felt really satisfied with their vocals, and wanted someone else to take the role onstage. When Simon received a call from Paul Rodgers broaching the idea of a reformation, it confirmed his belief that they'd broken up before they should have. At the very least, they could put the old band together again, if only just to undertake a farewell tour for all the fans who'd felt cheated by their sudden collapse.

Maybe it would be less temporary than that, for Paul was beginning to come to the same realisation as the others: that they were stronger together than apart. Conflicting egos and drugs had torn them asunder, but the damage need not be irreparable. Moreover, he still seemed to need the other three badly, and they felt some intangible obligation – maybe even a duty of care to their vulnerable guitarist – to try to put the clock back and rekindle the old magic that had brought them together. In 1972, the idea of rehab for recovering addicts was very much a thing of the future, and rescuing Kossoff from himself, they admitted, was the next best thing they could do. One valiant attempt had been doomed to failure. At around this time, roadie Jim McGuire visited Koss at his place at Golborne Mews, surrounded by pushers and other abusers, and was horrified by the pathetic state he was in. Jim and Andy agreed they had to get him out and stormed in one day, picked up his semi-comatose form, wrapped him in a blanket and drove him down to Surrey. After a few days of his kicking, screaming and demanding to be let go, they felt they could do nothing, so Koss left, returned to London and resumed his miserable way of life.

Later he admitted he never really wanted to reform the band after they split the previous summer, and the others 'sort of dragged me out of my pit'. Even so, with regard to reconvening all four, Andy said he was sure they all wanted to get back together again once they finally admitted it: 'What we'd had was better than what we were doing right then.' The reasons in favour were overwhelming, even if they decided it would be no more than a final tour and a thank you to the public, with all four members intent on pursuing individual careers afterwards. The news came out around the end of the year, with Glover informing the press before he told Blackwell, who was still hoping that the three splinter groups would somehow all establish themselves and make more money than one ever did. Yet as everybody else had realised by this time, none of them were likely to enjoy a fraction of the success that a reformation of the badly missed Free surely would. Island press officer David Sandison promised there would be dates in Britain, America and Japan. Afterwards, Paul Rodgers had plans to go to Muscle Shoals to record a solo album; Andy was planning a visit to Nigeria so he could study the world music scene; Paul Kossoff, he suggested, might be about to form a band with Traffic drummer Jim Capaldi to play a British and European tour, while Simon and Tetsu had been seen teaming up with Graham Bond for the odd gig, with a view to something coming from that. For all of them, the future was highly speculative.

On 23 January 1972, Free played their first gig since reforming, intended partly as a warm-up, at the Greyhound, Fulham. It had been confirmed only two days earlier, but even at that short notice it attracted over 2,000 fans – 400 more than the house record – for a 45-minute set featuring mainly the old standards. For the tour, they were intending to feature some new material as well as the old favourites, and also maybe record some shows for another live album – a plan that was scrapped because of a national miners' strike with subsequent power cuts throughout the country, sometimes lasting several hours at a time.

After a couple of days of studio time recording for the next album, the British itinerary began at Newcastle City Hall on 1 February with a sold-out and ecstatically received performance that finished with three encores. During the next three weeks, the tour went around the country, selling out everywhere, not least at Liverpool Stadium on 12 February where they broke the box office record previously held by Led Zeppelin. Everywhere Free went, the reception was ecstatic. Most tactfully overlooked that Koss' playing was often subdued and sometimes his guitar was out of tune, while on a personal level, Paul Rodgers and Andy spoke little to each other and were only seen together onstage. Andy said afterwards that it was as if the band was even bigger than it was before the split, and they found it difficult to handle.

The tour that had started so triumphantly ended less well. Plans for an American company to film one of the last shows (21 February at Newcastle) were disrupted by a warning of an impending blackout, so the band would have to be offstage by 9:00 p.m., and they cut their set short. They returned the following night so that fans would not be short-changed, and within a few minutes of starting, Koss collapsed. They had to ask the audience to keep their tickets and return for another show the following week: the earliest date that could be booked for them. The proposed replacement date was cancelled as he was too ill to make it, and was staying in London to recover. Plans for a free concert to make up for it, maybe at another local venue, fell through and were scrapped.

Throughout March and the beginning of April, the band returned to Island Studios for the fifth album. In addition to a few completely new songs, Paul brought 'Seven Angels' and 'Heartbreaker' from Peace's repertoire, while Andy came along with 'Travellin' Man' that had been demoed by Toby. Although both members wrote everything – some together and some separately – it was agreed that in order to seal their newly rediscovered (if fragile) unity and prevent any ill feeling, all writing credits would be shared equally among all four. Koss appreciated that the tour and album had been scheduled partly to help him recover from his depression and addiction, but the fact he was 'not that together', as he admitted, was hardly helped by the fact that he was yearning to play. But Andy and now Paul were contributing more keyboards and Mellotron than ever before, 'so that when it came to guitar, I didn't have a lot of spaces'. Richard Digby-Smith was in charge of the sessions, and found them some of the most tiring he'd ever done. There was an astonishing amount of attention to detail, and relationships between all four were hardly amicable. Paul Rodgers was particularly demanding and prone to losing his temper when things were not done exactly as he wanted.

The sessions and mixing were all completed by the beginning of April, when the band flew to America for the next tour.

Free: Free At Last (1972)

Personnel:
Paul Rodgers: vocals, piano
Paul Kossoff: guitar
Andy Fraser: bass, piano, Mellotron, acoustic guitar
Simon Kirke: drums
Producers: Free
Engineer: Richard Digby-Smith
Recorded at Island Studios, Willesden, January–April 1972
Release date: May 1972
Chart placings: UK: 9, US: 69
Running time: 36:38
All songs credited to Fraser/Rodgers/Kossoff/Kirke
Side One: 1. Catch A Train 2. Soldier Boy 3. Magic Ship 4. Sail On 5. Travellin' Man
Side Two: 1. Little Bit Of Love 2. Guardian Of The Universe 3. Child 4. Goodbye
Bonus tracks on 2002 CD reissue: Burnin' (Molten Gold), Honky Tonk Women (Mick Jagger / Keith Richards), Magic Ship (Alternative mix), Little Bit Of Love (Alternative mix), Guardian Of The Universe (Paul Rodgers solo version), All Right Now (Alternative take), Child (Early mix)

Free's fifth studio album opens with 'Catch A Train' – one of Andy's songs inspired by his giving directions to a friend (thought to be singer Robert Palmer, then a member of Vinegar Joe) coming from London to visit him at Woking – which makes a storming start, with a growling guitar riff and an impassioned soulful vocal. One of the most forceful tracks, it's followed by the less convincing 'Soldier Boy'. This song of Paul's inspired by the Vietnam War is given colour with some good, swirling keyboards and guitar, and a military drum rhythm. What lets it down is a rather overly simple lyric about the soldier boy standing on the battlefield under a red sky, hearing the bugle call, while people fall around him. It looks and sounds like an interesting idea that was simply not developed as far as it could've been.

'Magic Ship' is another of those songs that comes so near but again remains so far. Again, Paul's vocal is supplemented well by colourful guitar and keyboards, and also a distinctive hook. But once more, there is something too simple – even hackneyed – about the lyric, with its opening invitation 'Over there is my magic ship/Would you care to go on a trip?' In the right hands, and two or three years earlier, it could've made the beginnings of a good psychedelic track. As it is, there is a vaguely Procol Harum air to it. But in 1972, it had rather missed the boat (excuse the pun). Pursuing the nautical imagery, the mid-tempo 'Sail On' again has a very basic lyric, but after a simple opening with piano and tambourine, is enlivened by some excellent guitar played through a Leslie speaker, thus producing an almost Hammond organ-like sound.

'Travellin' Man' was Andy's song, the only number he wrote for Toby that he brought to the sessions. In his words, it was 'just a reflection of always being on the road, and the words just fitted the riff': the tale of a man who is always on the move, relishes his freedom and just loves to look up and see the stars above him. One of the most energetic songs on the album, it's a perfect match for Paul's gutsy vocal and the way Koss' guitar punctuates and curls around the spaces in between.

The album's single 'Little Bit Of Love' – a number 13 hit in the UK but a dismal 119 stateside – is a catchy song based around a cheerful chorus, with an interesting slightly slowed-down section in the verses and break, and features another superbly concise guitar solo.

'Guardian Of The Universe' is one of the most personal songs Free ever recorded. Paul had married Machiko Shimizu the previous year, and this was his ode to their son, Stephen. To some ears, it may sound mawkish, while others appreciate it for the sentiments towards his newborn child and his future. However, its recording created more discord between the band's two driving forces. Andy wrote in his memoir how Paul sang it 'and played some rather heavy-handed piano first', then asked Simon to add some drums. Andy thought the drumming was completely wrong – 'just totally inappropriate for this slow, beautiful song' – and told him he was murdering it. Every suggestion he made to try and soften it in keeping with the general sentiment was greeted with a cold stare and a response of 'Just play the bass and be quiet.' Paul's original idea had been to use just piano and a simple orchestral backing if possible, but it ended up as another band song, with piano and guitar filling in the spaces between lines.

At first listen, 'Child' might seem to be another song about fatherhood, but was actually written with Koss in mind, with its lines about life being a fairy tale, and how 'The clouds you're hiding behind in your misty mind, have disappeared'. A moody, subdued piece, it's built mainly around softly rippling piano and a gentle drum rhythm.

Appropriately, to close the album comes 'Goodbye'. In retrospect, this was surely Andy's parting statement to the group of which he'd been the self-appointed leader and – in effect – musical arranger: the musical equivalent of John Lennon's 'I want a divorce' from The Beatles. 'Is this how it's got to end?' the lyrics ask, 'But we've come to the end of our road together'. Slow and stately with the steady piano suggesting an Elton John influence, it sounds almost like a cry of pain with Koss' guitar sounding like it's screaming in anguish to enhance the melancholy.

Not for the first time, the cover design is basic, even uninspired. On the front is the title in garish balloon lettering more suited to a packet of sweets, and on the back, the basic information and individual shots of each member in the corner, all looking 'pretty shattered' in the words of Digby-Smith. As for the music itself, Simon said he thought it was one of their best albums with some excellent songs on it, while Paul went on record as calling it rather uneven. But the playing was difficult to fault, with keyboards providing much of the colour. And despite the sometimes pitiful state Koss was in by then, his guitar playing is still instantly recognisable. He said afterwards that he really enjoyed playing on the album, because during the making of the previous three, he'd been increasingly dominated by Andy, 'and I ended up playing what he wanted me to play'. This time he felt he was becoming more independent.

Yet too much of the music sounds plodding, restrained, and with a few exceptions, lacking in energy. The thought remains that what they needed was a tough, no-nonsense producer (and preferably another musician, or else somebody of the calibre of George Martin instead of a member of the Island top brass) who could call the two main sparring partners to order. Reviews were good, though they fell short of enthusiastic. To this day, the album has its fervent admirers among fans, who relish the more sophisticated sound and instrumentation, and the more mature, sometimes dark and doomy subject matter. At the same time, it has its detractors, who see it as uninspired, going through the motions, short on the gutsy blues foundations that had been Free's trademark, not really succeeding as a pop/rock album either, and even bordering in parts on a pretentiousness that did not really become them.

The American tour was planned to take in about 60 shows starting at the end of April, supporting acts such as Fleetwood Mac, The Faces and West, Bruce and Laing. At times it was a miserable affair. Koss' addiction had reached an alarming level, and only occasionally did he play onstage with anything like his old zest. Sometimes he was so out of it he seemed mentally in a different time zone, five minutes behind the others, while they tried to carry on, aghast but determined to make it work for the sake of their professional reputation. Several gigs were cancelled at short notice because he had been taken ill – in other words, was more or less comatose when it was time for them to go onstage. They were further disheartened when one of their roadies went to sleep in the back of the van and died from carbon monoxide poisoning due to a leak in the exhaust system. After that, the remainder of the tour was pulled while they returned to England to prepare for dates in Japan and Hungary. They held further rehearsals, with some more committed than others. Andy had had enough, and according to the press reports, in mid-July, he left the band. In his memoir, he said, 'It was my job to report that we'd broken up.'

The Japanese tour supporting Emerson, Lake & Palmer went ahead, mainly as Free were big business there, and to have cancelled it would've been financially ruinous for all involved. Koss was in no fit state to carry on, and had to sit it out. Rabbit was recruited on keyboards while Paul took over guitar in addition to vocals, with Tetsu standing in on bass, after the two new musicians had flown out to Japan for as much rehearsal as they could manage within the limited time available. Just before the first gig, Simon was rushed to hospital with suspected appendicitis and tonsillitis. Miraculously, medication and a good night's sleep enabled him to play, still unwell but capable of joining them for the first show. Once they were onstage, they could do no wrong, and the reincarnation of what some were dubbing 'The Paul Rodgers Band' went far better than almost anyone could've hoped. By the time they reached Hungary, tempers were beginning to fray between Paul and Rabbit, who was proving a little too assertive, and in his own words 'brash, loud and drunk', but they returned to England intact at the end of July. According to Simon, Paul's guitar work was 'a revelation, very sparse and soulful, and reminiscent of Albert King', though others considered it to be merely adequate.

In August and early September, rehearsals took place for a new British tour to last through until October, with dates in Italy and Romania to follow. Blackwell still regarded Free as the original quartet, and seemed to resent hired hands being brought in. But Glover, who had worked face to face with them on several tours, realised that the new band was working fine, and there could be no putting the clock back to a quartet in which the two main creative forces were barely on speaking terms. Koss was back on board, but still barely able to function. As they were getting ready to go on, Simon sometimes had to give him a crash course in how to play the songs on which Koss had shone only two years before; even showing him the chords to 'All Right Now' as he seemed unable to remember them. After the first few dates, the guitarist's performances were barely adequate, and Rabbit tried his hardest to cover up for him by taking a more prominent role on keyboards. On 15 September at Newcastle, they were setting the gear up for a soundcheck when Koss crashed to the floor with an epileptic attack induced by Mandrax withdrawal. He was rushed to hospital while that night's show and several subsequent dates were cancelled.

Though the obvious solution was for the rest of them to carry on with Paul Rodgers on guitar again, they had convinced themselves that the tour was the only thing giving their struggling colleague any motivation to stay alive. The truth was that while they strove to keep him in the line-up, he was in danger of dragging the band towards the inevitable point of no return.

Koss recovered enough to join them for some more studio sessions at the end of September. The British tour carried on the following month with more shows that underlined their pitiful decline, due entirely to his erratic behaviour and inability to function normally. When they played the Redcar Jazz Club on 12 October, he fell into the drum kit. Paul and Rabbit both lost their tempers and rounded on him in fury during the show: a scene that cannot have provided the audience with any pleasure. Afterwards, management informed them that after such an unprofessional display, they would never be booked there again, but it was an unnecessary ban as Free's clock was ticking. Eight days later, they played Newcastle City Hall. Koss managed to perform throughout, but from all accounts, he looked to be in a terrible state. Much as he adored and cherished his guitars, he ended up smashing the one he played that night into Rabbit's Hammond organ, breaking the guitar's neck in the process. It was a pathetic way to finish what they were unaware at the time was their last-ever British show.

The remaining few weeks of the year were taken up with further studio time. In September, they'd begun work on a chosen forthcoming single, 'Wishing Well': a song Paul Rodgers had written on the bass. As with the tracks on the previous album, though it was all his own work, he allowed all four musicians a co-writing credit. It was released on a 45 in December, entered the charts one month later and peaked at number seven in Britain in February 1973, and a modest 112 in America. A Bob Clearmountain remix was issued in Britain in 1985, returning the song to the top 100 for one week.

The work continued throughout December and Koss played on five tracks. But the others had already given him many chances and knew he could no longer be relied on. Sometimes in the studio, he really shone with a touch of the eager young guitarist he'd been at the start, but at other moments he was barely functioning. Fortuitously, Rabbit had an associate – guitarist William 'Snuffy' Walden – he'd known since their days in Texas together, and who had subsequently moved to London. On Rabbit's recommendation, Snuffy came and helped out. When Koss was in the studio at the same time, he seemed sufficiently alert to get quite upset at being so obviously supplanted. Ironically, both were credited as session musicians and not as members of the group (although Koss still appeared in the photo of the five-strong group on the album inner sleeve). Snuffy admitted he was just 'a hired gun', and the original founding guitarist had become increasingly semi-detached from the band he had helped form.

During December, Koss officially left; or rather, the band had left him. It has been suggested that he quit in disgust at being demoted to guest musician status, but the truth is more likely that he'd gradually distanced himself to the point where the others considered he had ceased to belong. Like Brian Jones and his negligible participation in the last Rolling Stones recording sessions he ever attended, Koss was barely contributing anything at all. While the others were hardly drink or drug-free at the time, they still managed to complete the work on schedule.

The album *Heartbreaker* was completed and mixed at the end of December, but when Blackwell heard the tapes, he complained they sounded too thin and were unfit for release. Andy Johns was summoned, and though he was about to leave for Jamaica to work on the next Rolling Stones album, he was asked to stay in England long enough to expedite a salvage job on the tapes so the record could be released as soon as possible.

Chapter Five: 1973

By the beginning of 1973, Free had become a fragile unit, barely holding together, clinging on to fulfil contractual obligations. An American tour supporting Traffic was scheduled to run through January and the first part of February, with a short British tour to follow after that. Snuffy was unable to commit himself, so again on the recommendation of Rabbit, a replacement guitarist for the live dates was found, in Wendell ('Del') Richardson from the Afro rock band Osibisa. Although his musical background was completely different, and Paul Rodgers was annoyed at having somebody who would not fit well foisted on them, there was no time to find anyone else. As diplomatic as ever, Simon – the other remaining core member of the original band – commented that the tour 'did stretch the bounds of credibility'. By adding Rabbit and Tetsu, they'd opened the door to other influences, even if their styles were not exactly suited to the music with which Free had always been identified.

As the two newest recruits, Tetsu and Del both felt like outsiders, and one was able to give considerable moral support to the other on tour. Del knew he never really was a part of Free, and was painfully unprepared for becoming a full touring member at such short notice. A few gigs into the itinerary, they awoke one morning to find that about 30 guitars had been stolen out of one of the trailers, and he was bitterly upset to find that a particularly prized instrument of his was among them. He cheered up when a music shop in New York heard an appeal broadcast on radio for its return, and generously invited him to come and take any Stratocaster from their wall, free of charge.

Even so, one morning mid-tour, Del told Tetsu that he intended to go home the next day as he was not comfortable with the band. Tetsu said he sometimes felt like doing the same, but urged Del to stick with it and see the job through. Del's wife promptly came out to join the entourage and give him some moral support. It did not escape the others' notice that almost immediately afterwards, Del began demanding more money. When Chris Blackwell asked Paul whether they were going to finish the tour with Del, Paul said he thought it unlikely. While Rabbit had no problems with Del as a person, he still bemoaned the fact that despite Koss' chronic unreliability, he was 'missing' him and they all wanted him there. It wasn't Free anymore, and Rabbit, for one, sensed the band was in its death throes.

Two gigs had to be cancelled when Paul sprained an ankle, so the tour was extended beyond the planned itinerary. As the unhappy saga wore on, Paul and Rabbit were increasingly at daggers drawn, leading to bitter punch-ups. The last show was at Hollywood Sportatorium in Florida on 17 February, and Koss turned up to – unknowingly – see their last rites, but hovered in the wings without making any effort to go and join them onstage. After they finished, Rabbit was enraged at the thought that the band he loved so much at first had turned into 'a travelling shambles'. He got thoroughly drunk, went into his dressing room full of mirrors – 'like a chorus girl's room', as he described it – and deliberately smashed each one. Blackwell walked in afterwards and calmly told him that he would be required to pay for the damage.

Free: Heartbreaker *(1973)*

Personnel:
Paul Rodgers: vocals, guitar, piano
Simon Kirke: drums, percussion, guitar
John 'Rabbit' Bundrick: organ, piano, backing vocals
Tetsu Yamauchi: bass, percussion
Additional personnel:
Paul Kossoff: guitar (Tracks 2–4, 6, 8)
Snuffy Walden: guitar (6–8)
Rebop Kwaku Baah: percussion
Producers: Free, Andy Johns
Recorded at Island Studios, October–November 1972
Release date: January 1973
Chart placings: UK: 7, US: 112
Running time: 35:45
Side One: 1. Wishing Well (Rodgers, Kirke, Yamauchi, Kossoff, Bundrick) 2. Come Together In The Morning (Rodgers) 3. Travellin' In Style (Rodgers, Kirke, Yamauchi, Kossoff, Bundrick) 4. Heartbreaker (Rodgers)
Side Two: 1. Muddy Water (Bundrick) 2. Common Mortal Man (Bundrick) 3. Easy On My Soul (Rodgers) 4. Seven Angels (Rodgers)
Bonus tracks on 2002 CD reissue: Wishing Well (US remix), Let Me Show You, Muddy Water (Alternative vocal), Hand Me Down/Turn Me Round (Bundrick), Heartbreaker (Rehearsal version), Easy On My Soul (Rehearsal version)

By the time of Free's farewell album, they had effectively become the Rodgers-Bundrick Band, no matter what Blackwell might've thought. In view of the tension between vocalist and keyboard player, it is perhaps remarkable (or says much for their work ethic and business sense) that

Above: Free in the summer of 1970, the year they broke through with 'All Right Now' and the album *Fire and Water.* (*Davidson Rockpix*)

Below: Bad Company in 1974, from an early photo session taken to promote the release of their eponymous debut album. (*Atlantic/Warner Music Group*)

Left: *Tons of Sobs*. Free's 1969 debut featuring a photograph taken in a graveyard in the Putney and Barnes area of London. (*Island/UMG*)

Right: *Free*. The sleeve of Free's second album, featuring a photo by Ron Raffaelli, has long been recognised as one of the classic 1960s record designs. (*Island/UMG*)

Right: *Fire and Water*. Following two non-charting albums, a number two single resulted in a number two album. (*Island/UMG*)

Left: *Highway*. The group and engineer hated the sleeve design, while some reviewers thought it was by a new group called 'Highway'. (*Island/UMG*)

Left: Free in 1969, a highly respected live attraction still in pursuit of a major breakthrough. (*Croydon Music Library*)

Right: Free on *Top of the Pops* in June 1970. Paul Rodgers sang 'All Right Now' live while the others mimed to the backing track.

Left: Simon Kirke and Paul Kossoff take a break between rehearsals. (*Croydon Music Library*)

Right: The sheet music to 'All Right Now'. Blue Mountain Music was established by Chris Blackwell in 1962, long before the Island label.

Left: A music press advertisement for Free Live in June 1971, released just as the group disbanded. (*Island/UMG*)

Left: *Free Live*. Paul Rodgers and several reviewers thought it their best album. (*Island/UMG*)

Right: *Kossoff Kirke Tetsu Rabbit*. Effectively a Free album without Rodgers or Fraser with vocals by Simon Kirke and keyboard player John 'Rabbit' Bundrick. (*Island/UMG*)

Right: *Free at Last*. The first album by the newly reunited group, with all compositions credited jointly to all four members. (*Island/UMG*)

Left: *Heartbreaker*. The group's farewell album recorded with help from guest musicians while they were slowly disintegrating beyond the point of no return. (*Island/UMG*)

Above: Free on stage 1971, shortly before the first split. (*Mike Hale*)

Right: The final incarnation of Free in 1972, with Paul Rodgers on guitar and Tetsu Yamauchi on bass. (*Croydon Music Library*)

Right: *Back Street Crawler*. Paul Kossoff's solo album, assembled mainly from jams in the studio, he said, 'really just a series of sessions with different people' (*Island/UMG*)

Left: *The Band Plays On.* Although nominally Paul Kossoff's band, much of the guitar playing was the work of Terry Wilson. (*Atlantic/Warner Music Group*)

Left: *Bad Company*. The first debut album by a British act since The Beatles to top the US charts. (*Atlantic/ Warner Music Group*)

Right: *Straight Shooter*. The second album was Mick Ralphs' favourite; 'big, roaring songs, all done more or less live'. (*Atlantic/ Warner Music Group*)

Right: *Run With the Pack*. According to Simon Kirke, it is 'a great album, but after that, the pace started to get to us'. (*Atlantic/Warner Music Group*)

Left: *Burnin' Sky*. The fourth album was released in 1977 to lukewarm reviews and failed to make the top ten in Britain or America. (*Atlantic/Warner Music Group*)

Above: Bad Company in 1976, the year they began by headlining the Great British Music Festival at Olympia, London. (*Davidson Rockpix*)

Right: Boz Burrell, whose first love was jazz, onstage with fretless bass, 1974 (*Mike Hale*)

Above: Bad Company onstage at the LA Forum on 16 May 1976, where they were joined by Robert Plant and Jimmy Page. (*Mike Hale*)

Left: An advertisement for the same gig where Bad Company played to a capacity crowd of 20,000 with Kansas as support.

Left: One of Bad Company's first major British dates was at Charlton Athletic football ground in London in May 1974, sharing a bill with The Who.

Right: Before Bad Company's honeymoon with the British music press was over, on the front page of *New Musical Express* in March 1975.

Left: Paul and Mick onstage at Earls Court in London in July 1977. They played there four nights in a row, their only British dates that year. (*Mike Hale*)

Right: Paul Rodgers who, by this point, was frequently playing guitar and keyboards onstage, with Boz Burrell. (*Croydon Music Library*)

Right: Bad Company in 1979, now unfashionable with the British music critics but still enthusiastically acclaimed by fans on their 16-date UK tour. (*Atlantic/ Warner Music Group*)

Left: *Desolation Angels*. Their fifth album was greeted as a return to form, including the single 'Rock'Roll Fantasy', the band's final major hit single in America. (*Atlantic/Warner Music Group*)

Right: Bad Company toured Britain in the spring of 1979. These would be their last dates in their home country until 1987, by which time Paul Rodgers had been replaced by Brian Howe, former Ted Nugent vocalist.

they stayed together long enough to complete an album, and ended up with the former singing two of the latter's songs. Others have said in retrospect that *Heartbreaker* was really another Kossoff, Kirke, Tetsu, Rabbit album, but with Rodgers this time.

Placed at the start of side one, 'Wishing Well' remains probably their most-loved single after 'All Right Now'. Despite a belief that Paul's lyric was directed squarely at his former guitarist, he insisted that it was about nobody in particular. Koss played on the single and album version, though Snuffy's guitar can be heard on a mix that was proposed for the American market but abandoned. Both takes are about the same length, but there is a noticeable difference in the intros, and also with Rebop's congas adding some sprightly percussion. The previously unreleased one appeared on a 12" picture disc in 1982.

'Come Together In The Morning' is one of those lyrics that could be addressed to a semi-estranged lover, or could be a general love-and-peace anthem of the kind that was so prevalent at the start of the 1970s. Organ and rippling piano dominate the backing, while Koss proved that he still had it in him to contribute a powerful guitar break when he stretched himself.

'Travellin' In Style' is a gentle, simple, country-tinged song with a pleasant tune, though it's lyrically and musically rather on the basic side, with the verses all on one chord. Kiki Dee recorded a cover version for her album *Loving & Free* later that year.

The title track almost marks a return to some of the best work on *Fire And Water*: an earthy number with more wailing guitar and keyboards to the fore.

Interestingly, this is more or less a record of two halves style-wise, with side one being the rock helping, and side two more in country and gospel rock mode, with two songs by Rabbit and the others by Paul. Rabbit's contributions – 'Muddy Water' and 'Common Mortal Man' – have something of a spiritual air about them, and inevitably are a showcase for the writer's keyboards as much as the singer's voice. As for the vocalist, his 'Easy On My Soul' follows a similar introspective path, while 'Seven Angels' has a hymn-like quality with Rabbit's organ giving a particularly strong flavour. At times, his work has a quality reminiscent of some of Al Kooper's work for Bob Dylan in the mid-1960s.

While Free may have ended their recording career some way from the blues, *Heartbreaker* is generally accepted as the second-best album they made. Though it was created at a time when they knew they were nearing the end of a tortuous road, it was to their credit that they ended their recording career on a positive note. The situation was in contrast to that of Creedence Clearwater Revival, who came to a dead-end in 1972 with a lacklustre and poorly selling album after the two remaining members had challenged the iron control of their frontman John Fogerty and demanded a chance to contribute some of their own songs. *Heartbreaker* was immeasurably better and more successful than Creedence's farewell *Mardi Gras*.

Once the American tour was over, there was no suggestion of any similar schedule in Britain. Irritated fans who wrote to the music papers asking why the American dates had been rearranged and cancelled while nothing was happening at home received no answer from the band or Island. Glover had repeatedly warned Blackwell – who steadfastly refused to get involved – that his star attraction was on the verge of breaking up again, and was so angry that he left the company. Five years after that first session at the Nag's Head, Free were *free at last* from each other: not with a bang, but a whimper.

Some 40 years later, Paul told Paul Elliott of *Classic Rock* that the way Free ended the whole saga was sad, 'but, looking back, we were babies'. Ironically, in hindsight, it was the two less-worldly 'country boys' who'd come from outside London who would prove to be the most determined to make it, and ended up staying together in an outfit that enjoyed lasting success, while their lead and bass guitarists would never regain such a high profile. Not only that, but Paul and Simon had been the two eldest members of Free, while in Bad Company, they were the two youngest.

'Travellin' in Style' was released as the album's second British single in March but failed to make any headway despite being chosen as the Radio 1 record of the week on the Johnnie Walker lunchtime show. Strangely, while it attracted little interest elsewhere, a push for 'All Right Now' a few weeks later met with more success. In July, Island took out advertisements in the music papers to announce that it was in the shops again – technically a new promotion with new stock, not a reissue as it had never been deleted, and the B-side and catalogue number remained the same. Three years after its initial blaze of glory, a return to the Radio 1 playlist helped to send 'All Right Now' back into the British charts with a peak position of number 15 on its second wind. In 1978 during the late 1970s craze in Britain for EPs in picture sleeves, it was born again as a three-track 45 with the full six-minute version on one side and 'My Brother Jake' and the previously unreleased recording of 'Wishing Well' on the other, and made it to number 11. In 1982, the EP was reissued as a 12" picture disc and reached the top 60 again.

In January 1991, a Bob Clearmountain remix, re-edited to the original four-minute single form, was issued to promote a new *Best of Free* compilation, and to coincide with a TV advert for Wrigley's chewing gum, putting the single in the chart for a fifth time, at number eight, with the 1969 John Peel session recording of 'I'm A Mover' on the B-side. As Island Records still owned the publishing rights, Paul had no say in the matter. In theory, he said, they were supposed to contact him to ask whether they could use one of his songs in that way, but they often did not, especially if the money was good enough. On one occasion, singer/vocalist and company exercised their joint power of veto. When the song was used to advertise a foot odour powder on TV – coming on 'to signify that your feet are All Right Now' – Paul rang Chris Blackwell to ask if permission had been sought: 'He had it taken off pretty smartly.'

After dissolving quietly, the former Free members took time out to consider their separate musical futures. In June 1973, Ronnie Lane left The Faces and Andy Fraser was asked to replace him, but declined, so Tetsu was invited and accepted. Andy had already formed the band Sharks soon after leaving Free the previous year. They released the album *First Water* in April 1973 and undertook a British tour, after which he left. The Andy Fraser Band released one further album and toured Britain, but found scant success. He continued to record sporadically and wrote several songs recorded by other artists – notably 'Be Good To Yourself' and 'Every Kinda People': moderate hits in the late 1970s for Frankie Miller and Robert Palmer respectively.

Rabbit remained much in demand as a session musician, especially for other artists on Island, and for the likes of Mick Jagger, Andy Fairweather Low and Joan Armatrading. He also played keyboards briefly with Mallard (formed by ex-members of Captain Beefheart's Magic Band) and subsequently joined The Who.

Although Koss was still functioning intermittently and unable to escape for long enough from the dealers who continued to keep him supplied, Blackwell gave him free studio time at Island, largely to give him a chance to focus on something other than his alcohol and drug consumption. Richard Digby-Smith helped him to put together material for a solo album, including various jams and tracks left over from previous sessions. Sometimes the guitarist would come in late at night on his own, and sometimes with other musicians, to jam and leave the tapes running. Through a combination of salvaged material recorded over the previous year and additional work done in the summer and early autumn, an album containing three instrumentals (one taking up a full side) and two vocal songs was completed, mixed and ready for release in November. As Koss said, it was 'put together rather haphazardly. It was really just a series of sessions with different people.'

Paul Kossoff: *Back Street Crawler* (1973)

Personnel:
Paul Kossoff: lead guitar
Trevor Burton: bass (Track 1)
Alan White: drums (1, 2)
John 'Rabbit' Bundrick: keyboards (1); piano, organ, chimes (4)
Alan Spenner: bass (2)
Jean Roussel: keyboards (2, 5)
Jess Roden: lead vocals (1); harmony vocals (4)
Tetsu Yamauchi: bass (3)
Simon Kirke: drums (4)
John Martyn: guitar
Paul Rodgers: lead vocal (4)
Andy Fraser: bass (4)
Conrad Isidore: drums
Clive Chaman: bass
Producers: Paul Kossoff, Bob Potter, Richard Digby-Smith, Jean Roussel
Recorded at Island Studios, mostly July–October 1973
Release date: 16 November 1973
Chart placing: Did not chart
Running time: 35:54
Side One: 1. Tuesday Morning (Kossoff)
Side Two: 1. I'm Ready (Jess Roden, Jean Roussel) 2. Time Away (Kossoff, John Martyn) 3. Molten Gold (Kossoff) 4. Back Street Crawler (Don't Need You No More) (Kossoff)
Bonus tracks on 2008 deluxe edition: Tuesday Morning (Early take 1), Tuesday Morning (Early take 2), Tuesday Morning Blues, Tuesday Morning Groove, Tuesday Morning Boogie, Tuesday Morning Piano Jam, I'm Ready (Take 4) (Jess Roden / Jean Roussel), The Lady Is A Tramp (Lorenz Hart / Richard Rodgers), I'm Ready (Take 10, Full version) (Jess Roden / Jean Roussel), May You Never (John Martyn), Leslie Jam (Kossoff / John Martyn), Time Away (Complete jam) (Kossoff

/ John Martyn), Molten Gold, Molten Gold (Songs of Yesterday version), Back Street Crawler (Don't Need You No More) (Single guitar track no. 14)

'Tuesday Morning' was over 17 minutes of one jam at Basing Street and was recorded mostly in one sitting in order to keep the spontaneity going, with the players just taking two short breaks. The rhythm section was Yes drummer Alan White and former Move bassist Trevor Burton, who had been jamming together for a while on a casual basis, though without any plans to take it further. Any ideas they might have had to do so were quashed when Burton joined The Steve Gibbons Band.

Koss launches it all with a few riffs while Rabbit fills the spaces in between on piano and organ. From about six minutes in, after a brief lull, they return with a chord sequence that echoes the intro to 'Fire And Water', playing variations on the theme for most of the rest. After breaking into a funkier rhythm another seven minutes after that, the mood quietens with carefully controlled guitar feedback, and a slow, stately four-minute section – even verging on ambient – reminiscent of Pink Floyd's style at the time.

The shortest track, at just over two minutes, introduces the second side. Jess Roden takes the vocal in 'I'm Ready': a snappy number that veers towards blues-based jazz funk. It's followed by 'Time Away': co-written with John Martyn. Island had sent him into the studio with Koss, Tetsu and Simon to record a new electric version of Martyn's album track 'May You Never', hoping it would be a hit, but it misfired and ended up as a lengthy jam session. This fairly slow instrumental is characterised by unmistakable tremolo guitar, with that slithery Latin American tone so beloved of Carlos Santana on some of his *Abraxas* album.

The second vocal track, 'Molten Gold' is a Free leftover, and not – as has sometimes been supposed – a brief reunion of the quartet. Originally titled 'Burnin'', 'Molten Gold' was written, rehearsed and partly recorded in March 1972 during the sessions that would result in *Free At Last*. Had it been completed and issued at the time, it would've allowed Koss a sole credit on a track by the old band: something that might've done wonders for his self-confidence. The presence of his former colleagues resulted in their inclusion on the rear cover credits.

To close comes the title track, which, according to his father David, had been written as a dismissal of the pushers, lowlifes and back street crawlers, telling them not to come hanging 'round his home anymore'. It had included a vocal track by Eugene Wallace that was, for some reason, removed at the final stages. After two quite slow numbers, it ends the album on a more upbeat mood with its honky-tonk-inclined piano runs and a powerful final note of tremolo guitar wizardry.

The two songs naturally relied on input from others. Basically, the album was something of a showcase to demonstrate that the guitarist was still an accomplished musician when he could focus properly, and when others could coax it out of him. It's an interesting collection, but is really more one for the Free completist than the average fan. The third and final disc of George Harrison's triple *All Things Must Pass* magnum opus consisted of lengthy instrumental jams and has often been held up as an example of the kind of record that only the most devoted fan is likely to play more than once. On balance, it does demonstrate rather more energy than *Back Street Crawler* – which sounds uncomfortably like a rather hit-and-miss collection, relying on the hope that the name on the cover would attract buyers.

Once the album was completed, everyone involved knew there was no prospect of Koss being in any state to take a band out on tour. As the full tracklisting above shows, there were many more fragments and even extended jams – one stretching out to nearly 40 minutes – that resulted in the release of a deluxe edition in 2008. But the original album met with indifference and never troubled the charts.

Its release in the final days of 1973 was followed by news in the music press that Koss, Andy Fraser, former Jimi Hendrix Experience drummer Mitch Mitchell and 'an unnamed vocalist' (who turned out to be Frankie Miller) were rehearsing with a view to playing gigs in the new year and possibly recording. That was as far as it went where Koss was concerned, though the Fraser/Miller partnership resulted in an appearance on *Top Of The Pops* with the top 30 single 'Be Good To Yourself' three years later.

Like the rest of his old bandmates, Paul Rodgers had been as concerned as anyone about the struggles of their guitarist and alarmed at the company he was evidently keeping. They still regarded each other as friends, and during the summer while his future was undecided, Paul invited Koss to his home studio where they recorded a few numbers. Paul also found himself on the music weeklies' news pages around this time after just one very non-committal phone call. Deep Purple were touring America and the ever-sparring vocalist Ian Gillan and guitarist Ritchie Blackmore were threatening to leave, or maybe fuelling an 'it's either me or him' saga. Ian (who did in fact quit at the time) later noted in his autobiography that plans were being discussed between him, drummer Ian Paice and Thin Lizzy's Phil Lynott, and 'Paul Rodgers was also in the frame somewhere'. Paul later explained that he received a call saying Ian was intending to quit and he was unsure what he was going to do next. So Paul thought about it, but on reflection, decided he would not fit in with Purple too well. It was no more than an idea blown out of all proportion. Many years later, it came to light that the three surviving members of The Doors had approached Paul to replace Jim Morrison, but at the time, he'd 'buried himself in the country', and they were unable to reach him.

Another member of a high-profile British band of the time was also preparing to move on. But his collaboration with Paul would come as little surprise, as the seeds of the partnership had been planted a couple of years earlier. Paul Rodgers had been through the learning curve of fronting a band that had scaled the heights, been let down by unsympathetic management, and capsized by musical differences, egos and drugs. Having drawn a line under Free – and under Peace, which had barely even registered on the radar – Paul was determined to learn from all the mistakes. He discovered a kindred spirit in Mick Ralphs of Mott The Hoople when the two not only met on tour in 1971, but also became close friends as they discussed songwriting, common aims and had the odd brief jam in the dressing rooms. Paul thought Mick had a very simple and effective guitar style, wrote a good song, and most importantly, seemed able to write the kind of material Paul could sing easily.

One of the songs they ran through just for fun was Mick's 'Can't Get Enough', which he'd recorded as a one-man demo, but one to which neither he nor Ian Hunter could really do justice. Mott had previously been quite a democratic band with Ian and Mick at the helm. But Mick said that since 'All The Young Dudes', it had increasingly been Ian's project, changing 'considerably over the years from a rock 'n' roll band to a Bowie-type product which I felt wasn't my bag'. Mick found it frustrating and hankered after 'something more bluesy, more simplistic, more earthy', closer to the sound of their first four albums. When asked about his guitarist's departure, Ian readily conceded that Mott didn't have a vocalist who could really do the songs the way they wanted, so Mick went and found himself a singer: the one he'd suggested – when on their tour with Peace – that they should try and recruit for Mott: 'He couldn't have really picked a better one, could he?'

Both men knew how much they had in common, though they had not necessarily decided at the start that forming a new band was the main intention. Mick realised that they would be ideal songwriting partners, especially as he thought Paul was much better working with somebody else as opposed to coming up with songs on his own and failing to produce sufficiently strong, catchy material. The partnership with Andy Fraser had flourished briefly, but soon been sundered by personal differences. But team Rodgers/Ralphs would be built on a more solid foundation.

Some years later, Paul explained to interviewer Rich Chamberlain that songwriting was in many respects the lifeblood of a band. When they first got together, both had some numbers ready, and then they collaborated on a few more:

> We would write together and separately, so we accumulated a lot of songs and we needed a band to put around those songs, and that's how that developed. Sometimes we would write together and that would maybe involve Mick writing the words and me the music or vice versa, or even a mixture of both. We'd fill in the gaps for each other when needed.

Mick's style was simple and very effective, and they just clicked as a partnership.

From further jamming sessions at Paul's house in Surrey, the idea gradually took shape. After Free had imploded, Simon Kirke took a complete break from music, spending four months in Brazil getting away from it all. He said it was 'a huge release when Free broke up' as the last few months had proven to be such a painful experience; he needed to leave it all behind him and have a complete change of scenery. On returning to England, he contacted Paul to find out what he'd been doing in the meantime. Paul invited Simon to his place, where he sat in on the jam sessions and was accordingly invited to be part of the new plan. Koss had remained a friend and came to join them a couple of times, but according to Paul, 'He just wasn't together,' while Mick was. When asked later about Mick, Koss was less than complimentary, saying that the former Mott man tried to rip him off with his playing style, and he wished he would do so better: 'His strings always sound so loose, like he's using rubber bands.'

Once the two ex-Free members and the soon-to-be-ex-Mott guitarist started rehearsing, it all gelled, and Kirke said that all they needed was someone else on bass. Alan Spenner – formerly with Joe Cocker's Grease Band – was initially invited but he turned up three days late for rehearsal, somewhat the worse for self-indulgence, and was not offered a second chance. Several others were auditioned or invited to audition, but all proved to be wanting: not least one who arrived at the station to be collected. When the others saw he was bald, they had second thoughts and drove away again. Meanwhile, Mott The Hoople were on tour in America, and at several hotels they stayed at, they were met with messages at reception asking their bass player Mr Peter Overend Watts to get in touch with Peter Grant at once. When he did, the message was 'The boys want you in the new group'. Realising that Mick was especially keen to recruit him, he said he was happy staying put, but promised to think about it. But everyone knew that he intended to stick it out with Mott.

Some way down the list was Raymond 'Boz' Burrell – a former vocalist and rhythm guitarist with The Boz People, alongside future Small Faces and then Faces keyboard player Ian McLagan. Boz had once been rumoured briefly as a possible vocalist for The Who when they thought Roger Daltrey was about to leave. He made several singles in the late 1960s under the name Boz and joined King Crimson as vocalist in 1971, also taking up bass guitar after Rick Kemp left to join Steeleye Span. Although the others were uncertain of him at first – King Crimson not having exactly been their style – he fitted in perfectly at their first rehearsal. Paul said, 'He had the ability to play it like a lead so that it covered a lot of ground, so it would lock with the bass drum,' and also flow melodically with what he and Mick were doing with the music.

For a band name, they considered Concrete Parachute, The Zoom Club and The Lounge Trousers, but settled on Bad Company. It was inspired partly by Paul seeing a poster for a spaghetti western of the same title (starring Jeff Bridges), and at the same time his memories of a picture in a book on Victorian morals that he recalled from his childhood – it showed a tramp-like figure with a bottle in his hand and a pipe in his mouth, while a small angelic-faced child looked up at him with interest; the caption below: 'Beware of bad company'. Grant and the rest of the management initially thought it was 'a terrible name', but as in the case of Free several years earlier, Paul and the band stood their ground. They defended it as not having any evil connotations but was meant in terms of being akin to the early American settlers: the men who had to be tough to survive. Beneath the no-nonsense exterior, they had their tender, emotional side, when they looked at the wonders of the land they had come to settle in and found it unexpectedly moving. Against that, there was no argument.

Notwithstanding the speedily resolved conflicts over their name, the band felt that strong management was important. As luck would have it, Led Zeppelin's five-year contract with Atlantic Records had recently expired, and they and their manager Peter Grant were planning to set up their own company: Swan Song Records. There was already a connection in that Clive Coulson, who'd been working for Free alongside John Glover as their tour manager, was now doing the same for Led Zeppelin. When he heard that Free was no more, he contacted Paul and advised him to contact Swan Song. They were keen to seek further signings and it was evident that The Paul Rodgers Band – as they had initially, if unofficially been known – would be a perfect fit.

Their association almost began with a major misunderstanding. Before Peter Grant had even heard a demo, they were told one day that he would come and sit in on a rehearsal. So they turned up, practised, practised, and went on practising. When he did not turn up after a few hours, they were furious that he'd let them down. After playing really aggressively at the end, they packed up in despair. When they went outside, they found that he'd been sitting there in his car all the time, listening and saying he enjoyed it so much that he didn't want to disturb them.

Once negotiations were completed, the next stage was to record that all-important first album. They rehearsed for about three months at Headley Grange, Hampshire, until they 'knew all the songs backwards', and then had an invitation to use Ronnie Lane's mobile studio there. Led Zeppelin had booked it, but their plans suddenly changed when John Paul Jones informed them that he was considering leaving. He had always believed that the group would be a short-term project, and now wanted to spend more time with his wife and young family, or – according to another sometimes-disputed story – take up a vacant post as choirmaster at Winchester Cathedral. The rest of the band and Grant urged him to take a little time off – 'you need to be not too well' being the official explanation, to quell music press speculation if needed – so he could reconsider his situation, and Bad Company reaped the benefit with some unexpected, instant studio time.

Paul and Mick had both come armed with several songs they'd been unable to use in their previous groups, and there was no shortage of material to choose from. Peter Grant offered them the chance to do some demos, but it took very little time to complete the first album, which they produced themselves with engineer Ron Nevison, who'd worked with Richard Digby-Smith as an assistant on sessions involving Peace, Toby,

Free, and also helping out Led Zeppelin. It took them ten days to get the backing tracks down, with Mick overdubbing his solos afterwards, and Paul his vocals, a little piano and occasional extra guitar.

The vocalist found it a particularly congenial album to record, saying that they had a great time because it was so communal. They slept in the same place where they were recording and set their equipment up in different rooms. Simon had his drum kit at the bottom of the stairwell 'for that big John Bonham sound', Boz standing next to him with a long lead plugged into his bass amp in the airing cupboard, while Mick and Paul would be playing guitars together in the sitting room with a couple of Marshall amps. On one or two tracks, Paul went outside and recorded his vocal on the lawn under a full moon, with the only ingredient missing being a dog howling in the distance. Every day they cooked in the kitchen, somebody would light the fire, they'd make tea and have breakfast, 'almost like a bunch of hippies there in the house'. Once everybody was up and ready, they would begin recording. Rather like The Band and Fairport Convention a few years before them, there was an aura of 'getting it together in the country' in the most relaxed surroundings imaginable. It made all the difference from the recording studios in London, which were a nightmare because of the logistics of getting everyone there on time, finding somewhere to park and always working against the clock.

Everything went relatively smoothly, with the album taking two weeks to record. Simon would never play a song more than twice. If they did two takes and it didn't sound right, it would be a case of 'Next song!' where the drummer was concerned, so they learned to nail everything in two takes. They liked to keep everything organic and basic, said Mick: 'We were all anti-synthesizers and drum machines and all that crap.'

The only real (albeit short-term) difficulty was unfinished legal business with Island, which delayed the release of the finished and mixed product until spring 1974. Although Free were no more, Paul and Simon still had their contractual commitments to the company, particularly the matter of cancelled tours that had incurred considerable costs. Island, therefore, retained the rights to release Bad Company's records in Britain and the first four albums and their singles appeared on the Island label in the home territory, Europe and Australia. Not until 1979 would their releases worldwide be on Swan Song.

Chapter Six: 1974

During 1974, Paul Kossoff worked sporadically at his music. Some around him thought he'd never really got over Free disbanding and was still feeling quite disorientated. He seemed to toy half-heartedly with the idea of putting a new band together, but the sessions with Andy Fraser, Frankie Miller and others proved to be unproductive, and it was obvious that any half-formed ideas of working together seemed unlikely to go further. After that, it was a matter of jamming and occasionally recording with the likes of Jim Capaldi, Amazing Blondel, Graham Bond, and on one memorable occasion, even Peter Green. Everybody who worked with Koss desperately wanted to help and get his career back on track, and when he was on form they all saw that on a good day he still had it in him. But he remained erratic, trapped in his drink and drugs hell, almost as if he was telling family and friends that he didn't want to be saved from himself. Every positive sign – such as a new live appearance supporting someone else, or news of an impending return to work and collaboration – was greeted with interest, if not delight and renewed hope of better things to come for the beleaguered guitarist.

But in the opening weeks of 1974, it was clear that this would be the year of Bad Company. As if to remind record buyers of the band they'd lost less than a year ago, Island released what would be the first of several compilations over the years. The double album *The Free Story* appeared in March, having been scheduled for October 1973 but delayed owing to an oil embargo led by the OPEC countries in the Middle East and a subsequent shortage of oil-associated products: notably vinyl for long-playing records. The record was ostensibly limited to a numbered edition of 50,000 copies, though unnumbered stocks were available for some time afterwards. Nevertheless, the 20-track collection – well packaged with a detailed biography from *Sounds*' Billy Walker stapled inside the sleeve; a previously unreleased Peace track; a number from Kossoff, Kirke, Tetsu and Rabbit, and the cream of Free's singles and album tracks – was quickly snapped up. Within a fortnight of release, it peaked at number two. The single album compilation *Best of Free* followed in America some months later.

Bad Company had a great deal to live up to, and some commentators thought they'd seen too many supergroups come and go, with sky-high expectations to be disappointed all too soon. *Time* magazine opined that this 'amalgam formed by the talented malcontents of other bands' would turn out to be 'a potent but short-lived rock phenomenon'. Yet in Britain and America, the band's first gigs and records were eagerly awaited. How could a line-up with their pedigree not deliver the goods?

A couple of warm-up gigs in Germany and Switzerland preceded a first British tour in March and April which began with an ecstatically received show at Newcastle City Hall on 9 March. Though they were bedevilled by sound system problems, a set consisting largely of numbers from the forthcoming album plus a few from the repertoires of their previous bands – such as 'Ready For Love' and 'Easy On My Soul' – kept the audience more than happy. Another song was 'The Stealer', which Paul had recently heard on the radio – not the Free version, but a cover by Bob Seger from his recent album *Back in '72*. Paul said he was so impressed with it that they stole the arrangement, although one would be hard-pressed to find any significant differences between the two versions.

On 11 April they played the Rainbow, London. Koss' girlfriend Sandhe said he went to see the show and stood in the aisles, but would not go to his seat. Once they stayed playing, he began crying, 'My brothers, my brothers,' and they both had to leave. According to journalist Steve Clarke, Koss had a rather different reflection, saying that he enjoyed the gig for what it was, 'though Mick Ralphs doesn't knock me out'.

The British dates wound up with an extravaganza at Charlton on 18 May 1974 – headlined by The Who, with Humble Pie, Lou Reed and Lindisfarne also on the bill. Though some fans were only there to see the main attraction, Bad Company played a well-received set that immediately won over the reviewers, with some of the band wondering if they really deserved the praise being showered on them from all sides.

One week earlier, the first single 'Can't Get Enough' was released in Britain, going on sale in America a month later. The song – with a guitar chord intro reminiscent of Mott The Hoople's 'One Of The Boys' – was the one Mick Ralphs had been saving up, and that Ian Hunter and Guy Stevens had always told him would be a sure-fire hit in the right hands. In *NME*, Steve Clarke proclaimed that unless The Beatles suddenly reformed, 'Can't Get Enough' would go down as the best single of the year. Mick remained quite modest, admitting that 'A lot of people got really excited about it. I couldn't understand what they were all raving about. It was a three-chord bash. It was only when Paul put his vocal on it that turned it into something a bit special.' He'd worked out a twin guitar solo which Paul asked him to demonstrate, and they recorded it live. Mick said that right at the end, there was 'a little discrepancy', which meant it was not note-perfect, but it still sounded so good that he suggested they keep it as it was.

Like the last Free single, it was chosen as a Johnnie Walker Single of the Week on Radio 1, and this time it made the Radio 1 playlist and a slot on *Top Of The Pops*, peaking at number 15 in the UK and number five in the US: their most successful 45 in either territory. Some four decades later, *Classic Rock* called it 'possibly the most played garage-band song of all time', as alongside The Beatles' 'Twist And Shout' and Lynyrd Skynyrd's 'Sweet Home Alabama', the three-chord intro was one of the favourites of young guitar players growing up in the 1970s.

In retrospect, with the exception of 'All Right Now', Free never really came up with a single that cut across the spectrum of pop and rock by being a record that appealed to rock fans but also instantly got people up on the dance floor. The Rolling Stones, Status Quo, Slade, The Sweet and others had done it several times already, and 'Can't Get Enough' instantly joined the list. Just two or three seconds of Simon's count-in – unannounced – and that distinctive double-slap on the drums was enough to get any club absolutely buzzing.

Bad Company: *Bad Company* (1974)

Personnel:
Paul Rodgers: vocals, piano, guitar
Mick Ralphs: guitar, keyboards
Boz Burrell: bass, backing vocals
Simon Kirke: drums, organ, backing vocals
Guest personnel:
Sue Glover, Sunny Leslie: backing vocals
Mel Collins: saxophones
Producers: Bad Company
Engineer: Ron Nevison
Recorded at Ronnie Lane's Mobile Studio, Headley Grange, November 1973
Release date: May 1974
Chart placings: UK: 3, US: 1
Running time: 34:45
Side One: 1. Can't Get Enough (Ralphs) 2. Rock Steady (Rodgers) 3. Ready For Love (Ralphs) 4. Don't Let Me Down (Rodgers, Ralphs)
Side Two: 1. Bad Company (Rodgers, Kirke) 2. The Way I Choose (Rodgers) 3. Movin' On (Ralphs) 4. Seagull (Rodgers, Ralphs)
Bonus tracks, 2015 reissue, second disc: Can't Get Enough (Take 8), Little Miss

Fortune (Demo reel 1), The Way I Choose (Demo reel 1), Bad Company (Session reel 2), The Way I Choose (Version 1 including false start), Easy On My Soul (Long version), Bad Company (Session reel 8), Studio Chat/Dialogue, Superstar Woman (Long version), Can't Get Enough (Single edit), Little Miss Fortune (B-Side of Can't Get Enough), Easy On My Soul (B-Side of Movin' On)

Bad Company had been given a remarkable build-up in the music press on both sides of the Atlantic, and it says much for the quality of their first album that it justified most if not all expectations. For a few weeks in 1970, Free had been placed on a pedestal as 'the new Rolling Stones', but soon crashed. But the band that rose from their ashes would not make that mistake. The full version of 'Can't Get Enough' – nearly a minute longer than the single, with another guitar solo after the final chorus and a conclusive ending instead of a fade-out – immediately established the sound of a confident new combination: their own masters, at ease with their music. With the Free albums, there was nearly always the sense that they were holding back, and for various reasons not quite achieving their potential in the studio. Now Paul and Simon had drawn a line under that, and with Mick and Boz on board, it was a fresh new start for everyone. Simon was convinced that he really progressed as a drummer on the album.

'Rock Steady' has a more bluesy vibe, but again a much more fully rounded sound than the old group achieved. 'Ready For Love' revisits a Mick song that he'd sung on Mott's *All The Young Dudes* two years earlier, but – as Mick was the first to admit – it took Paul's voice to do it justice. This time around, Mick adds some interesting, almost jazz piano fills towards the end.

Paul's soulful leanings would never be far away, and 'Don't Let Me Down' brings them to the fore. The mood is not far removed from the song of that title from the late Beatles era, and is driven by Paul's piano, with a lead break shared by Mick's guitar and a few lines of Mel Collins' sax, with a rich backing chorus from Sue and Sunny.

The title track was written by Paul and Simon, the latter adding some ideas of his own after Paul started it and got writer's block, after they had chosen the band name. Having a song that shared the band name seemed an interesting concept, and they penned a number about an outlaw: a gunslinger who was born with a six-gun in his hand, always ready to make his final stand. More piano and sparing but growling guitar add chilling colour to the tone of the lyrics. To Paul, the song had a rather western vibe, 'with an almost biblical promised land kind of lawless feel to it'.

'The Way I Choose' is another of Paul's returns to his soul roots, emphasised by Mel Collins' Stax-inspired horns and a rare appearance on organ and drums from Simon, while Mick's guitar adds a touch of an almost country waltz flavour. Although regarded as a rock guitarist, Mick's roots were as much in soul as those of Paul. Around this time, Mick remarked that his favourite guitarist and original inspiration was Steve Cropper, as he mused that sometimes they just wanted to be The M.G.'s with Otis Redding.

Mick had written and recorded 'Movin' On' with Mott The Hoople in 1972, as that elusive possible breakthrough-quality, hard rocking but still commercial hit, although it remained unreleased for ten years. He offered it to Island label mates Hackensack as a single later that year, and it became their only single before disbanding a couple of years later. It was a case of third time lucky when Bad Company recorded it, being just right for Paul's vocal. A regular live favourite, it gave them a second American hit early in 1975, though plans to release it as a single in Britain never came to fruition.

The album comes to a peaceful close with 'Seagull' – a solo tune for Paul with just acoustic guitar and tambourine, as he sings a peaceful song of freedom.

On release, the album received consistently good reviews, and from critics whose expectations had been high. In *Rolling Stone*, Bud Scoppa commented that it 'resembles Free in its structural starkness and early Mott in its stormy directness', adding that the rhythm section played with economy, 'but make up for the spareness of their lines through the sheer muscularity of their playing'. While Mick's songs contained nothing that hadn't been done a thousand times before, each still sounded 'irresistibly fresh', while Paul was one of the most impressive rock singers of the decade, sharing with Rod Stewart 'a vocal delivery that derives its expressiveness from a shifting emphasis on its jagged edge and its sweet, delicate centre'. Paul's dependence on his own writing or that supplied by other members of his bands for nearly all the material he performed, often 'forced him to make more out of the songs he sings than is actually there'.

Scoppa added that lack of consistently strong material may have prevented Free from making it in America, 'But fortunately, Mick Ralphs has as deft a touch with a rock 'n' roll song as he does with a guitar line.' That the new band's material was immediately perceived by many as far stronger, became self-evident when it was calculated that in Britain and

America, *Bad Company* outsold all Free's albums put together, and in America, went five times platinum.

As for Paul's own view, he was once quoted as saying that it was definitely their best album. Later he qualified his verdict by suggesting that it was very much a matter of opinion, but called it their 'most natural and organic album', when they were 'very raw, very fresh' and still did not really know each other very well. However, the chemistry had always been there. In particular, the combination of vocalist and guitar could hardly have been bettered. Simon said that nobody could've been further away from Paul Kossoff than Mick Ralphs, and they were not 'interested in any more geniuses'. Mick was great fun to be with and really brought Paul Rodgers out of his shell. 'By the end of Free, Paul had his back to the audience, he didn't want to know. Then Ralphs came along with his Max Wall impressions and the whole thing changed, and for the better.'

From June to September 1974, Bad Company toured America, aided by a massive publicity campaign, including posters on billboards throughout the land asking 'Does Your Mama Know You've Been Keeping Bad Company?' Initially, they either shared a bill with or supported the likes of Jo Jo Gunne, The Edgar Winter Group and Santana. Having started opening for other acts, they were soon headlining their own tour and were hungry to put their past behind them. Free had had a bad reputation among promoters because of the cancelled tours, but most were willing to accept that the member responsible for such a situation no longer had any connection with them. None of Bad Company had ever been well known as individuals in their own right, and at first, many of their American fans assumed they too were American. Having never had anything like the same reception with Free or Mott The Hoople, it was an astonishing experience that left the band wondering just how long it would all last.

Before the final show, on 10 September at the Music Ball, Boston, they were getting ready to go onstage when Peter Grant told them they were not going anywhere and called them sternly into a separate room. 'Is he gonna shoot us?' was their instant reaction. Instead, he pulled a large sheet off a table underneath which were four gold albums, one for each band member. Having genuinely had no idea of how well sales were going up to that point, they all had tears in their eyes, and Grant gave a short speech of congratulation, ending with 'Now get out of here and knock 'em dead!'

Three weeks later – on a front page sporting a photo of Paul Rodgers onstage and the headline 'TERRIFIC COMPANY!' – *Melody Maker* confirmed what a good year it had been for the band. In the paper's annual readers' polls, they were voted brightest hope; Paul was the top male singer in the British section, and 'Can't Get Enough' was the top single. They had ample cause to celebrate, as by good fortune, it was the week that the album topped the American charts (for one week), making them the first British group to do so with a debut LP since The Beatles. That same month, they took Ronnie Lane's mobile recording studio to Clearwell Castle, Gloucestershire, to record album number two. Next came a second British tour – from 28 November to 19 December – with Duster Bennett as support, including dates at Ipswich, Bournemouth, Hanley, Manchester, Liverpool and Glasgow, concluding with two nights at the Rainbow in London. For the time being, it was as if they could do no wrong on either side of the Atlantic.

Geoff Brown of *Melody Maker* was one of those who summed up the band's appeal and how they were the right band at the right time. They were, he said, 'essentially a mainstream band playing simple rock with power and dynamism, veering wide of the heavy-handed blitzkrieg of too many of their compatriot bands'. When they came along, they provided the perfect antidote to much of what was going on elsewhere in British music: 'the laughable pretence, the brainless banality'. Mick Ralphs cheerfully conceded that they knew that what they were doing was not 'particularly new or inventive, but it was a hark back to good, solid music that we all like'. Fans in their thousands on both sides of the Atlantic and beyond confirmed the band had got it right, and that with their first single and album, they had well and truly eclipsed the success of the first few releases by their previous bands.

Chapter Seven: 1975

Bad Company started 1975 with what would be their only British gig of the year: on 3 January at the Olympia in London. Their success had catapulted them into the high-earning bracket, and as tax exiles, they were only allowed to spend a limited amount of time each year in England. In February, they played four dates in Germany, but the majority of that year's live schedule was to be in America, with 18 dates spread over May and June. With their growing stature there – selling out 20,000-seat arenas in next to no time – Peter Grant was careful to help them preserve a certain mystique, and protect them from overexposure by restricting the number of interviews they gave to the media. One disgruntled journalist grumbled that they would end up following Led Zeppelin 'down the trail to where permission to speak is like a Nobel Prize for credentials'.

Prior to the tour, at the beginning of April, their second album hit the shops.

Bad Company: *Straight Shooter* (1975)

Personnel:
Paul Rodgers: vocals, piano, guitar
Mick Ralphs: guitar, keyboards
Boz Burrell: bass, backing vocals
Simon Kirke: drums
Producers: Bad Company
Engineer: Andy Johns
Recorded at Clearwell Castle, Gloucestershire, September 1974
Release date: 2 April 1975
Chart placings: UK: 3, US: 3
Running time: 37:08
Side One: 1. Good Lovin' Gone Bad (Ralphs) 2. Feel Like Makin' Love (Rodgers / Ralphs) 3. Weep No More (Kirke) 4. Shooting Star (Rodgers)
Side Two: 1. Deal With The Preacher (Rodgers / Ralphs) 2. Wild Fire Woman (Rodgers / Ralphs) 3. Anna (Kirke) 4. Call On Me (Rodgers)
Bonus tracks, 2015 reissue, second disc: Good Lovin' Gone Bad (Alternate vocal and Guitar), Feel Like Makin' Love (Take before master), Weep No More (Early slow version), Shooting Star (Alternate take), Deal With The Preacher (Early version), Anna (Alternate version), Call On Me (Alternate take), Easy On My Soul (Slow version), Whiskey Bottle (Early slow version) (Rodgers / Ralphs / Burrell / Kirke), See The Sunlight (Previously unreleased) (Rodgers / Ralphs), All Night Long

(Previously unreleased) (Rodgers), Wild Fire Woman (Alternate vocal and guitar), Feel Like Makin' Love (Harmonica version), Whiskey Bottle (B-Side of Good Lovin' Gone Bad)

Straight Shooter is, to some extent, a continuation of the first album, but with perhaps a small degree of further sophistication, veering towards what would later be recognised (sometimes dismissively) as AOR music or stadium rock. Some critics have seen it as moving away a little from the more blues-based style of Free: traces of which lingered on the debut album. But there is still a freshness about it – the union of four musicians still having a ball as they jointly created the music they'd been longing to make for some time. Most importantly, for a new band, following up a five-times platinum album (US sales) was never going to be easy. But they had the talent and the quality material to deliver another massive seller, and one that many critics believed was the equal of – if not even better than – the first. In the end it went three times platinum in America. Both went gold in Britain.

Those wanting a worthy successor to 'Can't Get Enough' found it in the opening track: Mick's 'Good Lovin' Gone Bad'. After they had the first hit, Mick recalled that everyone said to him, 'Write another one!' His reply was, 'What do I do, play it backwards?' The song he brought them was arguably the most powerful, musically heavy number they ever recorded. Paul's vocals stop short of the masterful controlled screaming that Robert Plant and Ian Gillan had made their own, but he pours every bit of soul he can into these lyrics about a passion that has turned sour, while Mick's guitar is a masterclass in controlled aggression. There is an interesting moment of light and shade in the subdued lines between the main verses and chorus. Released as a single ahead of the album, it met with only moderate success, reaching number 31 in Britain and 36 in America.

Having found it difficult to choose the album's first single, they were unfazed by its comparatively low chart placing. Mick was content that it sold for a couple of weeks until the album was available, when people started buying the latter. This was obviously what they wanted, especially when everybody recalled that Mott had struggled for even one British top ten LP and never came close in America. Bad Company, he admitted, did not need to worry too much about Britain in terms of 45s. To him, the scene seemed very narrow in terms of singles and how governed it was by *Top Of The Pops*: 'If you don't fall into that format, then your single doesn't stand much of a chance.'

Far more successful was the album's classic moment of tenderness 'Feel Like Makin' Love'. Tasteful acoustic guitar chords introduce a song that came about as a Mick and Paul collaboration, with tenderness in the verses that explode into an all-systems-go climax for the chorus. The last of three British hit singles for the band – reaching number 20 here and number ten in America – it always remained a favourite onstage. An alternative version with Paul adding harmonica remained unissued for many years. In the 21st-century live incarnation of Bad Company, the song was rearranged to feature latter-day member Howard Leese's mandolin and Paul's harmonica in the break, adding an irresistible folk-rock flavour reminiscent of vintage Lindisfarne.

Having made several somewhat unheralded contributions to the Free albums, Simon steps into the spotlight with two compositions of his own on this album. The first – 'Weep No More' – is given the full treatment, with the intro a sensitive strings arrangement by Jimmy Horowitz that slides seamlessly into a mid-tempo rocker with piano and organ equally to the fore behind Paul's vocals, while guitar takes centre stage in the main break. Simon referred to it as his 'first really good song'.

Though it was never released as a 45, 'Shooting Star' reviewers singled the song out as being the album's finest six minutes, and in retrospect, it is sometimes regarded as the best track to which they ever put their name. Paul becomes the acoustic singer-songwriter, while the band provide sensitively muted accompaniment as he sings the story of a schoolboy inspired by hearing The Beatles' 'Love Me Do' – picking up a guitar himself and telling his mother that everything is going to be fine as he embarks on his new life: forming his own rock 'n' roll band, making a record that hits number one, but then being found dead in his bed with an empty whisky bottle and tablets found beside him. Paul insisted that it was something of a cautionary tale, carrying a warning of excess and the general casualties the music world had claimed in recent years. There was, however, a sense that the fates of Jimi Hendrix, Janis Joplin and Jim Morrison had provided some inspiration – all people that were hugely talented but like moths to a flame: 'The idea that they were shooting stars came into my mind.' All of them were in a business where they were meant to be having a good time, 'and most of the time we are, but a lot of people aren't making it through'. Within a year of the album's release, the fate of Paul Kossoff gave the song added poignancy: Koss' demise naturally affecting Paul and Simon deeply. Yet there is a note of consolation in the line that ends the final verse – an assurance that the music lives on: 'If you listen to the wind, you can still hear him play.'

Paul was singing some of the verses of that song in the airport as they were about to fly to America for the second tour. He had the guitar on the plane with him and was working actively on it as they flew over the Atlantic. It had all started with the line 'Johnny was a schoolboy', and thinking, 'That's a good song.' At first, he wondered where he'd heard it before, and when he realised it had been only in his own imagination, he immediately grabbed pen and paper to write it all down, and it just flowed out of him.

'Deal With The Preacher' – a song that had been in their live set from the start – benefits from the same effective touch as 'Good Lovin' Gone Bad'. From the opening guitar intro, it storms along at full throttle for much of the way, but with a more measured, calmer interlude.

'Wild Fire Woman' stands out with a slightly funkier rhythm, guitar complemented by organ, and above all Paul's chorus high notes which stop just short of a controlled scream. Had they been looking for a third single, this would've been an obvious choice.

Originally recorded on *Kossoff Kirke Tetsu Rabbit*, Simon's 'Anna' is next. It follows the same arrangement as the original, and is exactly the same length. While it was the drummer's song, there's no denying that Paul's vocal outranks his, driven by electric piano and the most sparing hint of electric guitar. Simon modestly felt that his vocal on the previous version had never done the song justice, and he was more than happy for it to be revived here.

The six-minute epic 'Call On Me' continues the first album's tradition with a peaceful song with prominent electric piano in the backing. On first listen it sounds a trifle bland, but improves on closer acquaintance. In the instrumental coda, the bass line has a touch of The Beatles' 'While My Guitar Gently Weeps', with a relaxed solo from Mick over the top.

When they recorded the first album, Paul said they were 'very raw, very fresh', and hardly knew each other. Once they'd done a tour together, 'it was a different band really': they'd moved on and knew each other as people much better. Reaction to the new album was almost on a par with the unanimous approval that greeted its predecessor. Interviewed some years later by Mick Wall, Mick Ralphs acknowledged that their first three albums were the best: a verdict that is hard to contest. *Straight Shooter* was definitely his favourite: 'Big roaring songs, again all done more or less live. We'd just come off the road and we would still be on fire.'

In an interview with Kevin Cooper, Simon agreed, saying it was the album that showed they were 'not a flash in the pan'. Just about every rock critic was lining up to pay their compliments. In *NME*, Roy Carr praised Bad Company for their honest-to-goodness rock, saying that it was 'a most apt title for four blokes free from access and pretensions. Can you think of a better way than having a good time?' He also suggested that a shortened 'Shooting Star' would've had great potential as a single.

The album release was followed by a tour of America throughout May and June, starting on 9 May at the Lakeland Civic Center, Florida, with a final show on 20 June at the Forum, Inglewood, California. One further date that summer was a festival at the Roman Theatre of Orange, France: a three-day event from 15 to 17 August, promoted as 'the French Woodstock'. Bad Company played an 11-song set on the first day, topping a bill that also included fellow Island acts Fairport Convention and The Jess Roden Band. After 'Feel Like Makin' Love' had given them another top ten American single, they toured with Styx, whose tour manager told them, 'The guys come to see Styx, and the women to see Bad Company.'

After that, they prepared for the third album: to be recorded at Grasse on the French Riviera. As Ronnie Lane's mobile recording studio was unavailable, they booked The Rolling Stones' Mobile Studio. At the first house they chose, the equipment truck was too wide to negotiate the narrow roads and bends, so they had to rent another more accessible venue nearby, which turned out to be a farmhouse. Despite various other hazards – including Simon falling off a motorcycle and injuring his arm, and neighbours arriving with guns to make them stop at intervals as they were making too much noise in a normally quiet neighbourhood – the album was completed on schedule.

Meanwhile, the tragic saga of Koss – his substance abuse issues and plans with other musicians that barely got past the starting line and would lead to a sadly predictable conclusion – continued to unwind, but not before another band was put together. Terry Wilson-Slesser, vocalist with Beckett – a band that supported Free on some of their final British shows and then also disbanded – was recruited alongside two old friends of Rabbit: bassist Terry Wilson and drummer Tony Braunagel. Having worked with him before, Koss was keen for Rabbit to join them, but he was already committed to session and tour work with others, so the other two recommended Mike Montgomery to bring them up to strength.

All the musicians knew that for all his musical prowess when functioning properly, Koss had a poor reputation when it came to reliability. But after a few rehearsals in the spring of 1975, they felt the project had a good chance of working. They moved out of London for a while, to Sawmills Studio near Fowey, Cornwall (far away from evil temptation and Koss' *friends* in the capital) where they could do some recording and rehearse for a nine-date tour to take place in May and June. Afterwards, when they returned to Olympic Studios to complete the album, Koss quietly escaped from the studio to get his fix from a nearby acquaintance. He was soon found, dragged back, and – against the odds – the project was swiftly completed. Once they'd decided on a band name – and what better than the one Koss had used for his solo album – the tour was finalised. Some of the performances were erratic, but fans were so thrilled to have their guitarist back – when for a while it had seemed he was in irreversible decline – that he still received an ecstatic reception.

Atlantic Records immediately showed interest and a contract was signed. The album was scheduled for release in September and another tour of Britain was arranged, starting with a free show at Hyde Park in London, and then to Belgium for a warm-up before the British dates. Before any of it could happen, Koss was taken ill and rushed to a clinic with a stomach ulcer. When his condition deteriorated and he fell into a coma, he was rushed to hospital, suffered a cardiac arrest and was clinically dead for 35 minutes. He was revived but remained in a coma for the next 24 hours. After being discharged and told firmly that he needed to behave more sensibly in the future, as his body would not give him another chance, he was sent to a health farm to recuperate. The tour was cancelled and he appeared briefly in an interview on BBC TV's *The Old Grey Whistle Test*, looking plainly unwell.

The Band Plays On was released in November, but to no tangible fanfare, sales or interest beyond Koss' most fervent followers. Back Street Crawler played four dates, at Liverpool, Glasgow, Newcastle and London, most of which were little short of disaster due to Koss' incoherent behaviour.

Back Street Crawler: *The Band Plays On* (1975)

Personnel:

Paul Kossoff: lead guitar

Terry Wilson-Slesser: vocals

Terry Wilson: guitar, bass

Tony Braunagel: drums

Mike Montgomery: keyboards, vocals

Additional personnel:
Pete Van: baritone saxophone (Tracks 7, 9)
Eddie Quansah: trumpet, flugelhorn (7, 9)
George Lee: flutes, tenor and soprano saxophones (7, 9)
Producers: Back Street Crawler
Recorded at Ridge Farm, Sawmills, Olympic and Basing Street Studios, summer 1975
Release date: November 1975
Chart placings: Did not chart
Running time: 44:16
All songs written by Mike Montgomery unless stated otherwise.
Side One: 1. Who Do Woman (Back Street Crawler) 2. New York, New York 3. Stealing My Way (Mike Montgomery / Paul Kossoff) 4. Survivor 5. It's A Long Way Down To The Top
Side Two: 1. All The Girls Are Crazy 2. Jason Blue 3. Train Song (Terry Wilson / Tony Braunagel) 4. Rock & Roll Junkie 5. The Band Plays On (Terry Wilson)

Back Street Crawler's debut album had its roots in the blues, but also owed more to a funkier brand of American hard rock with the occasional nod to soul. Some claimed to hear a Free influence in their sound, alongside that of Humble Pie, The Doobie Brothers, Spooky Tooth and others. Paul Kossoff is credited as lead guitarist, but how much he can be genuinely credited as a member in his own right, and how much of the lead guitar was actually the work of Terry Wilson, is anyone's guess. On 'Stealing My Way' – which has traces of Free about it – he receives a co-writing credit with keyboard player Mike Montgomery, who was responsible for writing six tracks on his own, and whose organ work is a strong component of every song. The feeling remains that Koss' creative input throughout was not that significant. Guitar solos are a vital component of each of the ten tracks, as might be expected, but Terry was partly – if not largely – responsible for them. The opening track 'Who Do Woman' – credited to all five – settles quickly into a funk-rock groove, with a touch of The Doobie Brothers' 'Long Train Runnin'' or Led Zeppelin's 'Trampled Underfoot', and doesn't really deviate from the pattern, while the slower second track 'New York, New York' is a moodier, world-weary song, with echoes of The Band's 'The Weight'.

The more up-tempo material is balanced out by a couple of slower, reflective numbers. 'Jason Blue' probably deviates more from the pattern than everything else, starting as a laid-back number with a hint of Steely

Dan that nods to a jazz feel, gathering pace after about a minute when the drums kick in, and then veering towards early Chicago territory once the horn section dominates. 'Train Song' is notable for a flowing Carlos Santana-style lead break, while 'Rock & Roll Junkie' – the second track to use a brass section – tends to bring AC/DC to mind.

While the album is, on the whole, a worthwhile listen, the lack of any really strong commercial song with a suitable hook to grab the listener and scream 'potential hit single!', did not help its chances. The failure of Koss' solo album and the earlier *Kossoff Kirke Tetsu Rabbit* to chart at all, rather confirms that the British rock guitarist, who fans desperately wished would slay his demons and enjoy the glittering post-Free career he needed, would never attract substantial album sales on the strength of his name alone.

Chapter Eight: 1976

For Bad Company, 1976 opened much as the previous year did, with a gig at Olympia in London. This time they were heading the three-day Great British Music Festival, and on 3 January, they topped a bill that also included fellow Swan Song signing The Pretty Things, Be-Bop Deluxe, Ronnie Lane's Slim Chance and Nazareth. Bad Company's 14-song set gave the audience a first chance to hear numbers from the new album *Run With The Pack*, including the title song 'Sweet Little Sister' and 'Young Blood'. The rest of the set was made up of tracks from the first two albums plus 'The Stealer': the only surviving number from Free days.

In *Sounds,* John Ingham said they stole the show and were obviously the only band who came across as really comfortable in the place. According to Geoff Brown in *Melody Maker*, they had the best sound of the day, the music was direct and punchy, and he opined that while there was nothing innovative about their music, 'on his night, Paul Rodgers is a colossal performer'. The only negative note came in *NME* from Chris Salewicz, who admitted to finding their records 'successful but very boring', and commented that their performance was so lacklustre and predictable he almost walked out. Nevertheless, most of the other scribes were united in their approval, and it proved to be a suitable curtain-raiser for the imminent album.

By this time, there were stirrings of a backlash against Bad Company in their own territory. Success would inevitably lead to a reaction, with detractors coming out of the woodwork, some of them critics doubtless ready to knock them as British superstars who had deserted their country's fans in pursuit of the dollar across the Atlantic. But as they readily pointed out, it was the fans who loved the music and paid to come and see them – not the journalists with their complimentary tickets – whose opinions really counted.

Bad Company: *Run With The Pack* (1976)

Personnel:
Paul Rodgers: vocals, piano, guitar
Mick Ralphs: guitar, keyboards
Boz Burrell: bass
Simon Kirke: drums
Producers: Bad Company

Engineer: Andy Johns
Recorded at Grasse, France, September 1975
Release date: 21 February 1976
Chart placings: UK: 4, US: 5
Running time: 36:14
Side One: 1. Live For The Music (Ralphs) 2. Simple Man (Ralphs) 3. Honey Child (Rodgers / Ralphs / Burrell / Kirke) 4. Love Me Somebody (Rodgers) 5. Run With The Pack (Rodgers)
Side Two: 1. Silver, Blue & Gold (Rodgers) 2. Young Blood (Jerry Leiber / Mike Stoller / Doc Pomus) 3. Do Right By Your Woman (Rodgers) 4. Sweet Lil' Sister (Ralphs) 5. Fade Away (Rodgers)
Bonus tracks, 2015 reissue, second disc: Live For The Music (Take 1 alternate vocal and guitar), Simple Man (Take 3 early mix), Honey Child (Early mix, alternative guitar solo), Run With The Pack (Extended version, alternative vocal), Let There Be Love (Take 1, previously unreleased) (Ralphs), Silver, Blue & Gold (Take 1, Early mix), Young Blood (Alternate vocal), Do Right By Your Woman (Alternative vocal), Sweet Lil' Sister (Live/Studio backing track), Fade Away (Early mix, Alternative guitar solo), Do Right By Your Woman (Acoustic version), (I Know) I'm Losing You (Studio jam) (Norman Whitfield / Edward Holland Jr. / Cornelius Grant), Young Blood (Alternative version 2), Fade Away (Island Studios demo)

Run With The Pack was the third Bad Company album to be released in a little over 18 months, and it would've been remarkable if it had been the equal of its predecessors in quality. The consensus of critical and fan opinion at the time and retrospectively suggests that it fell a little below the standard of the first two. On the basis of their both being five-star collections (or at the very least four and a half), *Run With The Pack* probably rates four. But two years of almost incessant touring had prevented them from having adequate time to replenish their catalogue of material (and perhaps the lack of another knockout single).

It begins with 'Live For The Music' – a fitting statement of intent, but it still lacks the impact of the opening songs on the first two albums. The musical foundations rest largely on a funky, single guitar chord, from which the basic tune deviates little. Boz adds a disco-flavoured bass line that fits in well, and Mick's guitar solo takes flight and screams out suitably from about halfway through. After about three minutes, both frontmen fade out and it shuffles along with just bass and drums until they too fade after nearly another minute. It stayed in the live set for a short time, but was soon dropped, though reinstated some years later.

'Simple Man', a more folky, mainly acoustic song in similar mode to 'Ready For Love', eases the pace. The lyric is the message of a yeoman working on the land, with freedom being 'the only thing that means a damn to me'. On a musical level it works well, though it attracted some criticism at the time from reviewers who thought such a song rang a little hollow from a band whose tax-exiled members were living privileged lifestyles as they moved between concert stage and luxury hotel suite.

'Honey Child' takes them back into full throttle. One of the strongest cuts on the record, with an instant hook and infectious chorus slightly reminiscent of 'Good Lovin' Gone Bad', it might've made a much better start to the album. A distinctive, slightly distorted guitar intro for a song about a young femme fatale, it makes more demands on Paul's voice. It became the second American single, though only charted at number 47.

While Bad Company were hardly the typical 'love songs' band, 'Love Me Somebody' proved they could work in the genre as well as anyone. A subdued waltz that tells of a crush from schooldays and the crazy fool who used to follow his loved one home every day hoping she would at least say hello, finds Paul's soulful vocal backed mainly by piano and organ, with sparing lead which Mick described as his 'smooth and creamy' style. This is probably the best song of its kind from the whole of their catalogue.

Appropriately, the title track is probably the most adventurous on the album. At nearly five and a half minutes, it's also the longest, and experiments with faster verses and the choruses dropping to half time, concluding with a tasteful string arrangement. Paul wrote the song on the piano, and for him the strings had always been an important part of the song. Jimmy Horowitz came to the recording session with a small portable tape recorder, and while the track was playing, he asked Paul how he wanted the strings in the background. Paul immediately sang it and Jimmy went away to score it accordingly. A couple of nods to Beatles lyrics – 'You never give me my money, you won't even see me' – might also raise a knowing smile. The track was released as a single in Britain (but not America). In fact, it was the only British single, though it tanked, and the band would never have another hit 45 at home.

Although little heralded at the time, 'Silver, Blue & Gold' is another of those songs that later went on to reach overlooked classic status. A reflective, acoustic love song with prominent dobro and piano, a strong hook in the chorus and one of Rodgers' finest uncharacteristically mellow vocals supplemented with harmonies, this sounds at times more like early Eagles or one of Rod Stewart's folk-rock tunes. Simon later commented that they never saw themselves as a singles band – 'a hangover from Zeppelin' – and Peter Grant was not keen on the idea either. But when Atlantic Records head Ahmet Ertegun told Peter that this song ought to be put out as a single, he tried to persuade the band to do so.

The track that did receive that honour in America was the very different 'Young Blood': the only cover they ever put on an album (excluding one snatch of singalong, more of which later). The old Coasters song – beloved of The Beatles in their early days, and later given a new lease of life in 1971 by Leon Russell and friends at the concert for Bangla Desh – by Bad Company standards was almost a novelty number. Although they never regarded themselves as a singles band, while they were recording the album, it dawned on them that there was no obvious track yet to release as a 45, and Boz suggested they ought to try recording the old Coasters favourite. They camped it up a little with the call-and-response lines 'look-a-here' and 'what's your name'. Live audiences and American radio loved it straight away, and it became the first American single, reaching number 20.

'Do Right By Your Woman' (another leftover from the unissued Peace songs in 1971) is another country-flavoured ballad, with shining vocal harmonies, acoustic guitars and harmonica. In order to capture a different atmosphere, they initially recorded it live around a campfire. As the fire was sparking and crackling with some vigour, they decided it was probably not good enough for use in that form, so they recorded a cleaner version in the studio. The outdoors one appeared some two decades later on a compilation.

A swift return to no-nonsense rock 'n' roll then comes with 'Sweet Lil' Sister'. The Rolling Stones' 'Dance Little Sister' or even Mott The Hoople's 'Drivin' Sister' may come to mind. It's a fine rocker with a gritty rhythm guitar that may be predictable, but in the best possible way.

Finally, another ballad comes with 'Fade Away'. Gentle piano chords, a prominent bass line and strings accompany a world-weary song in which Paul sings 'High adventure I've just begun/Fame and fortune got me on the run'. Coming as the album's parting shot, was this an acknowledgement that the endless rock-star routine – studio/album/tour and downtime in hotel rooms with all creature comforts there for the asking – was beginning to wear a little thin? The band photo on the inner gatefold – showing them unsmiling at the camera as they chill out on a sofa, with drinks and cigarettes in hand, and Bugs Bunny on the TV screen in front of them – suggests an air of jaded ennui.

Despite one or two weaker moments, *Run With The Pack* holds up as a very fine album, only marginally behind its two predecessors. Looking back on it, Simon said he saw it as the third in a triad of albums that he thought were 'among the finest in rock 'n' roll', while conceding that the standard of material on subsequent albums wavered from brilliant to dubious. Reviews were generally favourable if not ecstatic, although Pete Erskine in *NME* scathingly considered that their popularity was testament to 'just how conservative the mainstream *progressive* fan really is', suggesting that much of it came over as a cross between a poor man's Stones and Free. For him, the two opening tracks reminded him strongly of Led Zeppelin and Crosby, Stills, Nash & Young respectively, while 'Sweet Lil' Sister' sounded like 'Elton trying to photocopy the Stones again'.

The first few weeks of the year were also a busy time for Back Street Crawler, although time was running out for their guitarist. Several dates were set up in America for February 1976 and, as they had worked together before, Koss decided he wanted Rabbit in the band, much to the anger of Montgomery who thought it nothing short of a slap in the face after the hard work he'd already put in. At the same time, it dawned on Atlantic Records that they had paid an enormous sum of money for a new band whose leader was a total liability. John Glover was still managing them but also losing his patience, and during an argument in the studio one day, Koss tried to attack him with a bottle, resulting in a fight that left Koss with two broken fingers and subsequent inability to play his guitar for a while without splints.

Making the best they could of an impossible situation, with pending American dates already scheduled for February, the band went into the studio to try and give Koss something to focus on as much as anything else. Snuffy Walden was called in again and played most of the guitar on the sessions, while Koss' contribution was minimal: 'Koss came in and basically rolled through the tapes, though I can't say he seemed too interested,' Snuffy commented afterwards. Koss' presence was restricted to one recording session at the last possible moment. Digby-Smith recalled having to lean him against the amps and put his guitar in his hand, and they had to stay there until the job was done. It took the whole night and into the morning as they coaxed the notes out of him, after which they walked out into the glaring sun, exhausted at the end of the session.

As for the tour dates, Snuffy played as his ability to play like Koss had been proven in the past, while Koss would come onstage as the group's MC, welcome the crowd, introduce the musicians and then stand or sit at the side of the stage. If he felt inclined, he would join them for an encore of 'The Hunter' or 'All Right Now'. It was an oddly haphazard attitude, but by this stage little more could be expected of him. On some dates, the audience booed, hissed and demanded their money back, and one promoter refused to let the band remove their equipment afterwards until they returned part of the fee. Koss didn't turn up at all some nights, and they would have to go onstage without him. He'd plainly lost interest in being part of the group, let alone leading it.

One brief flash of light in a dark life came when Bad Company were playing the consecutive nights of 2 and 3 March at the Los Angeles Forum, while Back Street Crawler were headlining four nights at the Starwood Jazz Club nearby. Matters were arranged so that Paul Rodgers and Simon would go to the Starwood after Bad Company's show had finished and join Back Street Crawler onstage for a finale. They jammed on a few old blues classics and Koss seemed close to his old form. But these would be his last shows ever.

A 20-date British tour was arranged to begin on 25 April, and the album – recorded so quickly – was ready to be mixed and rush-released to coincide with the tour. Koss – whose role on it had been limited – was unhappy with it and told the others that when they returned to London: 'I don't think I'm gonna be doing this any more.' The band arranged to fly from Los Angeles to London for rehearsals, making a quick stop at New York on the way. On 19 March, during the first leg of the journey, Koss' body gave up the fight, with 'cerebral and pulmonary oedema' being cited on the death certificate. The album was released a month later, but the British tour with the up-and-coming AC/DC as support – due to begin on 25 April – was cancelled, and the band continued as Crawler. Atlantic dropped them and they signed to Epic. They made two more albums that similarly received scant attention except from the faithful and disbanded in 1979.

Peter Grant broke the sad news by telephone to Simon straight away, suggesting it would be best to withhold it from Paul for a while as it might throw the next few dates of Bad Company's American tour into jeopardy. A few days later, Paul's then-wife Machiko rang him and said he needed to know at once, otherwise he would only find out the hard way. His first impulse was to get on a plane and go straight home, but he was persuaded to complete the tour and realised it would be more professional to do his grieving in his own time after that.

About three years later, Simon said the death of their former guitarist marked the moment when Free were really finished: 'Up until then it had always been maybe we'd get back together properly.'

Back Street Crawler: *2nd Street* (1976)

Personnel:
Terry Wilson-Slesser: lead vocals
Terry Wilson: bass, acoustic and electric guitars
Paul Kossoff: lead guitar
Snuffy Walden: lead guitar (Uncredited)
Tony Braunagel: drums
Producers: Back Street Crawler
Engineer: Richard Digby-Smith
Recorded at various New York studios, January–March 1976
Release date: April 1976
Chart placings: Did not chart
Running time: 37:32
Side One: 1. Selfish Lover (John Bundrick) 2. Blue Soul (Terry Wilson) 3. Stop Doing What You're Doing (Back Street Crawler) 4. Raging River (Terry Wilson) 5. Some Kind Of Happy (Terry Wilson)
Side Two: 1. Sweet, Sweet Beauty (Terry Wilson) 2. Just For You (John Bundrick / Dean Rutherford) 3. On Your Life (John Bundrick) 4. Leaves In The Wind (John Bundrick / Dean Rutherford)

Back Street Crawler's album sounds rather like a pale shadow of the first. Having to entice their lead guitarist into the studio at all, just to give him one reason less to go on the hunt for more dubious substances, was never going to be conducive to recording a world-beater. There is the same continuation of competently-played hard rock meets funk, taken at varying speeds, and the odd hint of Steely-Dan-inspired rock with jazz at the edges. Again, none of the songs really stand out, sounding lacklustre and forced as if merely to fulfil contractual obligations and no more. There is little more to be said about a record where everybody is going through the motions with minimal inspiration. It was clearly never going to succeed where the first one had failed.

Bad Company toured America extensively from March to May 1976, promoting their album. According to journalist Mick Wall, if there was 'a singular event that would put the stamp on Bad Company's US coronation', it was a gig on 16 May at the Los Angeles Forum. That night, with Kansas as support, they played to a crowd of 20,000, and after the finale of 'Bad Company', they were joined onstage by Robert Plant and Jimmy Page for a jam comprising 'The Train Kept A-Rollin'', 'You Shook Me', 'Bring It On Home' and 'I Just Wanna Make Love To You'.

Although they were ready for a break at the end of the tour, management persuaded them to carry on, and with barely a pause they returned to France, where they began work on the fourth album. As the music world was increasingly aware, rock bands who had held the critics in the palm of their hand three or four years earlier could not take this for granted any longer. Events would prove that the major names of their ilk would hold on to their fan bases and continue to sell albums and tickets just as well as before, particularly in America. With the stirrings of punk rock in London – soon to spread throughout Britain – Bad Company, Led Zeppelin and their fellow tax exiles were soon to become desperately unhip among some sections of the media.

A close listen to some of the tracks on *Run With The Pack* had suggested that Boz was as ready to experiment as anybody else. Having originally come from a jazz background and then played with King Crimson (the uncrowned kings of prog rock), with his fretless bass, Boz was one of those players who relied on intuition rather than technique and was open for any new challenges. It was reported that at one point around this time, Paul – an accomplished if unheralded bass guitarist himself from several years back (though his skills had rarely been needed since he helped form Free) – once picked up Boz's fretless instrument so he could have a go and put it down a few minutes later with a shake of the head.

Some years later, Simon said that, in retrospect, he always thought the first three years of Bad Company were the happiest of his life. The money was great, they were feted wherever they went, and they were backing it up with talent and great shows. But after that, they were on 'that carousel of album/tour/album/tour', and it began to grow stale for them.

While everyone appreciated and recognised the need for Bad Company to experiment a little rather than just recycle past glories ad nauseam, when they went into the studio once more, they knew they were not ready to get back on the treadmill again. To their credit, there would be one or two surprises on the album. But instinctively, they knew they couldn't deliver a blinder every single time. At least they had a few months respite from touring, with no dates for the last few months of 1976 and nothing more until May 1977. Even so, for nine years Paul and Simon had been in bands that were committed to being out on the road much of the time, and still writing songs for the next album. At the time, they thought it was the norm, but only later did they realise what demands it was making of them.

'By the time we got to do *Burnin' Sky*, we'd just done a four-month tour and we were basically shagged, to be honest,' Simon admitted. They had peaked with *Run With The Pack,* and it was the beginning of the end. 'I think after that, the pace started to get to us.'

According to Mick, 'When we came to the fourth album, we found we hadn't got any ideas, we were floundering; we managed to cobble *Burnin' Sky* together. We realised we might've been having too much of a good time and not doing the job.'

Chapter Nine: 1977

Entering the studio less well prepared than usual, Bad Company recorded several rather out-of-character tracks that must've startled listeners on first acquaintance. It was clearly not what fans expected, and was by some distance the least successful of their 1970s albums. Paul later admitted that while they were recording, at one point, they found it such heavy going that they thought since they had started it they would finish it, but probably not release it. Nevertheless, 'As it turned out, it wasn't a bad album.' Posterity has to agree with their verdict. It might be more accurate to say that, in places, it doesn't sound completely like the Bad Company of the first three albums. But since *when* was trying to break new ground instead of repeating yourself ad infinitum a bad thing?

Bad Company: *Burnin' Sky* (1977)

Personnel:
Paul Rodgers: vocals, piano, guitar, accordion
Mick Ralphs: guitar, keyboards
Boz Burrell: bass
Simon Kirke: drums
Additional personnel:
Mel Collins: saxophone, flute
Tim Hinkley: keyboards
Producers: Bad Company
Recorded at Château d'Hérouville, France, July–August 1976
Release date: 3 March 1977
Chart placings: UK: 17, US: 15
Running time: 44:47
Side One: 1. Burnin' Sky (Rodgers) 2. Morning Sun (Rodgers) 3. Leaving You (Rodgers) 4. Like Water (Rodgers / Machiko Shimizu) 5. Knapsack (The Happy Wanderer) (Friedrich-Wilhelm Möller / Antonia Ridge) 6. Everything I Need (Rodgers / Ralphs / Burrell / Kirke)
Side Two: 1. Heartbeat (Rodgers) 2. Peace Of Mind (Kirke) 3. Passing Time (Rodgers) 4. Too Bad (Ralphs) 5. Man Needs Woman (Ralphs) 6. Master Of Ceremony (Rodgers / Ralphs / Burrell / Kirke)
Bonus tracks, 2017 reissue, second disc: Burnin' Sky (Take 2, Alternate vocal and guitar), Morning Sun (Take 3, Early version), Leaving You (Take 1, Alternative vocal), Like Water (Take 1, Rough mix), Knapsack (The Happy Wanderer) (Early run-through), Everything I Need (Take 2, Rough mix), Peace Of Mind (Alternate

version), Passing Time (Alternative vocal), Too Bad (Full Version), Man Needs Woman (Alternative Vocal & Guitar), Too Bad (Early version, Mick Ralphs vocal), Man Needs Woman (Take 2, Early version, Mick Ralphs vocal), Burnin' Sky (Take 1, Alternative vocal), Unfinished Story (Previously unreleased)

The title track was developed from an idea that Paul had written in a Paris hotel the day before they were due to go into the studio, and as they had only recently come off the road, he needed some songs at once. He'd already worked out the chords for a chorus and part of a verse. When they entered the studio, they hit the record button, counted it off and they started singing 'The sky is burnin'', and he made up the lyrics on the spot, recording them all in one take. It's an atmospheric piece, bookended by thunder crashes, with restrained but menacing guitar that lets rip with fury during the break, otherwise complementing the lyric's dark narrative mood. It tells the story of a fugitive from justice, running underneath a burning sky with guns and dogs on his trail until he's apprehended while swimming across the river, and ends up before a judge who says he will lock him up and throw away the key. Released as a single in America, it peaked at number 78, their lowest chart position of the Paul Rodgers era.

There is no such drama on 'Morning Sun' – the mainly acoustic love song of a man who is at peace with the world, and completely mesmerised by the sunlight in his lover's eyes. A tender guitar is complemented by the soft tones of Mel Collins' flute. 'Leavin' You' suggests a throwback to the general sound of Free. Howling bluesy guitar adds the main spark, and calls to mind the general flavour of 'The Stealer'.

'Like Water' – written by Paul and his then-wife Machiko Shimizu in the Free days – is the last of the Peace songs to be revived by Bad Company. Relaxed organ, guitar and a simple, effective bass line are the perfect complement to lyrics like 'My soul is a stream on the water'.

Eighty seconds of daftness follow in the shape of 'Knapsack (The Happy Wanderer)' – an old Austrian folk song that, as Simon admits, they did 'one drunken evening, so we were scrabbling for ideas'. It was not listed as a separate track on the label of the original vinyl release, or on the inner sleeve, and the gatefold cover deliberately omitted all information except for the band name and title, but it was separate on CD reissues from 1994 onwards. Moving swiftly along, to end side one comes 'Everything I Need': one of only two tracks credited to the whole band. It sounds very much like something out of the 1960s, with a three-chord pattern reminiscent of 'Louie Louie', Paul sounding almost like

Buddy Holly, and after one chorus, a brief spoken interlude: 'Baby, when you wrote that letter…' – something so beloved of Elvis Presley, several other rock 'n' rollers, and more recently, British glam rockers like The Rubettes and Mud. As the album's British single, it was ignored by radio and sank without trace.

Continuing the vintage rock 'n' roll theme on side two comes 'Heartbeat', sharing a Buddy Holly title, though, of course, a different song. Slightly funky in rhythm, Boz's bass line is a particularly strong factor on this one.

Simon's sole contribution comes next with the laid-back 'Peace Of Mind'. Enter Paul Rodgers the soul singer again, with a short spoken intro addressing people searching for peace of mind and chasing rainbows, who never find true reality as they have their heads in the sky. Mick's flowing guitar solo and stately organ add to the mood. A similar flavour follows in the next track, 'Passing Time', with its philosophical theme of how 'passing time brings a wiser mind', in helping one to see the things they never saw before.

Anybody longing for a return to the heavier Bad Company of old will find it in 'Too Bad'. This is another nod to Paul and Simon's days in Free, with sharp, insistent, bluesy guitar riffing topped off with a powerful solo. The mood persists in 'Man Needs Woman' – a gutsy three-chord rock 'n' roll tune in the best Rolling Stones or Status Quo tradition, with Paul's vocal coming close to that inimitable controlled scream, and belting sax work towards the end.

The greatest surprise comes in the last seven minutes with 'Master Of Ceremony': the second number credited to all four. A few seconds of reverse tape flow into a deliberately muddy-sounding jazz/blues jam of mostly organ, bass and drums with the occasional flash of guitar and saxophone. As for the song itself, it's more a stream-of-consciousness rap – a thinking aloud session asking people to choose their own direction in life, as people have got to learn to live together, no matter what their differences, be it the colour of their skin, their political stance, or whether they like to walk, ride, fly or take the train. Paul sounds quite unlike himself, as if his vocal is being beamed in from another planet, and there is something strange and unworldly about the track. This is Bad Company's 'Tomorrow Never Knows' or their 'Strawberry Fields Forever', almost.

It would not have been surprising if some had hailed this album as a step forward: a determination to not continue serving third-rate rehashes of old ideas. But it was as if everybody evidently wanted more of what they had before, and reviews were lukewarm at best. Simon admitted that 'the critics rounded on us and we paid the price', with *Melody Maker* heading their appraisal, 'A Crack in the Sky'. The album entered a musical world where the tried and tested still ruled the album charts as before (ABBA, Pink Floyd, The Eagles, Fleetwood Mac, plus TV-advertised compilations by The Shadows and Frank Sinatra), but the cool names – in Britain at least – were The Clash, The Stranglers and The Sex Pistols: all of whom had yet to release their first albums.

Wisely, Bad Company took time out after the release of *Burnin' Sky*. Simon admitted it was not really a very good album and paled beside the standard of the first three: 'Four years at that pace was like eight at any other pace.' Although they had some good songs – padding it out with some substandard material written on the fly, a directionless jam and a drunken campfire folk song – all suggested that Bad Company were running out of inspiration. Boz later told Chris Welch of *Melody Maker* that 'Our bottle had gone and we were killing ourselves, so we knocked it on the head. We could have carried on working forever at that pace.'

There were no lengthy tours to sell the album to the masses. In May, they played three dates across America, their first for almost a year, and in July, their itinerary comprised three shows at Earl's Court in London, followed by two further weeks of dates in America later that month. The musical climate stateside was less volatile, but in Britain the punks had become the critical darlings in certain sections of the music press. Led Zeppelin and Bad Company – relegated to the 'old farts' list – both suffered a backlash from some of the more hip journalists. Paul admitted that they were unaware of this at the beginning, as for them, 1976 was their *tax year* out of Britain: 'It wasn't just the brain drain, it was the rock 'n' roll drain as well.' They were abroad and 'punk happened underneath that'. He never liked nor understood it. When asked if it made him feel like the music they were playing at the time had become outdated, he replied that it was not the case in America, but in England: 'Overnight we were sort of dinosaurs.'

Nevertheless, changing their music in any way never crossed their minds, and being unfashionable had no effect on ticket sales in London. As Simon pointed out, 'It's the fans that count, not the rock critics.' Punk was a kick in the backside to them, and he praised The Clash and The Damned as good bands but was not enthusiastic about The Sex Pistols:

'Rock 'n' roll is just a musical vehicle for rebellion and that was theirs.' He never really liked it, and while it shook up some of the more established names, 'We just got on with it.' He told Vivien Goldman of *Sounds* that punk bands would not last very long, only while the music papers were championing them before they moved on to the next fashionable craze: 'I don't think they have the talent or the inspiration that will make them endure.' Even the Pistols were not universally praised by their peers. Captain Sensible of The Damned once said how disappointed he was when he first heard 'Anarchy In The UK', as it sounded to him like Steptoe (the 1960s sitcom icon portrayed by Wilfrid Brambell) backed by Bad Company.

Paul shared Simon's views, admitting that he neither liked nor understood the new genre. He told Chris Welch of *Melody Maker* that there were some good bands – notably The Boomtown Rats (who, Bob Geldof admitted, were pop rather than punk) – but on the whole, he thought it was not good for music: 'It was destructive without offering an alternative.' While Bad Company were always open to fresh musical ideas, they never aimed to set themselves up as spokesmen for the new generation. Above all, Paul firmly believed that they should never bring political issues and 'all that depressing stuff' into their music. He liked the lyrics to say something, but it was not his intention to change the world overnight: 'Something simple and understandable that people can relate their own experiences to.' The last track on *Burnin' Sky* had hinted at politics but in an idealistic, non-specific manner.

Chapter Ten: 1978–79

For Bad Company, 1978 would be a completely gig-free year, although they returned to work during the summer. That August, they regrouped at Ridge Farm Studio in Surrey. While they had all benefited from a break, general disenchantment was beginning to set in. Paul felt Mick was not contributing enough, and it was significant that of the ten songs selected for the album, five were written by the vocalist and only three came from the guitarist, the other two coming from Boz: one all his own work, and the other a collaboration with Simon.

However, Paul had recently embraced, with some excitement, one of the wonders of modern technology: one of the first models available of the newly developed Roland guitar synthesizer. Being so fresh and relatively untested, it was very unreliable. Paul said, 'It was all right if you didn't touch it or move it,' which sounds somewhat self-defeating for a musical instrument. There was no chance of taking it on tour, as it was liable to cut out, but it gave a magnificent sound in the studio, and when he played the chords, it sounded like nothing they'd heard before: like a rock 'n' roll fantasy, in fact. From that came the idea for the title of a new song: an anthem that expressed Paul's feelings about everything in rock 'n' roll: 'I wanted to cover the whole spectrum, particularly that rock 'n' roll was a magical illusion of colour, sound and light.'

By the time the second US tour came along and their second album had made it in America, the band and Peter Grant – keeping their eye on the rapidly changing British music scene – knew that the key to lasting success was to concentrate their efforts on live work there. As Simon explained to Penny Valentine in *Creem* in 1979, their music had always been blues-based, influenced by American musicians. Much was expected from them in Britain at the start of their career, and while they lived up to those expectations, things then changed radically, particularly from the perspective of a media too keen to jump on a new bandwagon and dismiss everything that came before as ancient history: 'The music was in a state of constant flux, still is: from glitter to punk, punk to new wave…' Where did they fit into the picture? 'Permanent wave,' he replied.

Though the band and their manager had previously attached little importance to singles, they appreciated that times had changed. The once hallowed and later humbled 45 rpm disc was now no longer regarded as the preference of only teenagers, and had achieved a new respectability of sorts in the punk and new wave era. But Paul was aware that by the late 1970s – while the old guard of rock 'n' roll hadn't been completely banished to oblivion by punk rock or disco, and could co-exist quite happily alongside both – 'You needed a couple of singles anyway from a record to make it really kick in.' The Swan Song label and its flagship act Led Zeppelin had generally been dismissive towards releasing 45s, for reasons of both economics and image. But they saw that the music industry changed from year to year, and in the summer of 1979, the label was about to enjoy two major British hit singles with one of its few successful newer signings: Welsh rock 'n' roller Dave Edmunds. He was never a strong album seller, even though he became the only act other than Led Zeppelin (plus solo ventures by Plant and Page) and Bad Company to give Swan Song any British album chart entries, modest though they might be. Like it or not, by the end of the decade, the power of singles as a major marketing tool to benefit album sales was entrenched more firmly than ever, with singles nay-sayers like Led Zeppelin and Rory Gallagher more in a minority than ever.

By autumn 1978, Bad Company's *Desolation Angels* (taking its name from a Jack Kerouac novel) was recorded, mixed and ready for release early in 1979. As their deal with Island had now expired, it was their first worldwide release on the Swan Song label.

They returned to Britain for 16 dates between February and April 1979, which included Newcastle, Birmingham, Glasgow, Southampton and Wembley. Afterwards, one of the band's entourage – who'd previously been uncertain whether they'd be welcomed with open arms after having been away from Britain for some time – told the press it had all gone much better than expected. They seemed to be attracting 'the denim-clad army who go for bands like Deep Purple and AC/DC'. There was nothing to worry about, despite the occasional grumble when asked why their music was still the same, to which Boz retorted, 'Because we don't want to play in 11/7 time to please a bunch of intellectuals.'

Paul loved it when audiences included a healthy contingent of enthusiastic headbangers seemingly intent on impersonating each member of the band, calling it 'fantastic'. At a gig in Edinburgh, he remarked that, 'The atmosphere was so strong that you couldn't help but play well. That's why I don't take the bad reviews too seriously.' The critics could knock them, 'but if bands like us disappeared, they'd really miss us'.

Paul also relished his role of being more of a musician onstage, instead of just the frontman wielding the mic stand most of the time. When he also played guitar and keyboards on certain numbers, it was much more interesting for him and was also good for filling out the overall sound. He admitted he was not really a virtuoso on either, but 'It's not just singer and band all night.' Over the years, he'd also learned the importance of restraint and accepting his place: 'I assumed that if you had to play guitar, you have to turn the volume up: dreadful mistake. Mick is the lead guitarist, full stop, and I throw in a few licks when I get the chance.'

Bad Company: *Desolation Angels* (1979)

Personnel:
Paul Rodgers: vocals, guitar, piano, synthesizers, harmonica
Mick Ralphs: guitar, keyboards
Boz Burrell: bass
Simon Kirke: drums
Producers: Bad Company
Recorded at Ridge Farm Studio, Surrey, August–September 1978
Release date: 17 March 1979
Chart placings: UK: 10, US: 3
Running time: 41:03
Side One: 1. Rock 'n' Roll Fantasy (Rodgers) 2. Crazy Circles (Rodgers) 3. Gone, Gone, Gone (Burrell) 4. Evil Wind (Rodgers) 5. Early In The Morning (Rodgers)
Side Two: 1. Lonely For Your Love (Ralphs) 2. Oh, Atlanta (Ralphs) 3. Take The Time (Ralphs) 4. Rhythm Machine (Burrell / Kirke) 5. She Brings Me Love (Rodgers)
Bonus tracks, 2020 40th anniversary edition, CD1: Smokin' 45 (Alternative version 1), Smokin' 45 (Alternative version 2), Rock Fever (Outtake), Oh, Atlanta (Slow version with Fender Rhodes), Rock 'n' Roll Fantasy (Alternative version 1), Rock 'n' Roll Fantasy (Alternative version 2), Rock 'n' Roll Fantasy (Alternative version 3), Crazy Circles (Alternative version),
CD2: Gone, Gone, Gone (Alternative version), Early In The Morning (Alternative version), Lonely For Your Love (Alternative version 1), Take The Time (Alternative version 1), Evil Wind (Alternative version), Take The Time (Alternative version 2), Lonely For Your Love (Alternative version 2), She Brings Me Love (Alternate version), What Does It Matter (Blues jam), Rhythm Machine (Alternative version), Amen (A cappella)

Heralded as a return to form, and an album that the band admitted was much better than its predecessor, *Desolation Angels* was in part a skilful welding of two genres. At the end of the 1970s, several rock acts – like Rod Stewart, The Beach Boys, The Rolling Stones and Electric Light Orchestra – had realised that not only was disco music not going to go away, it took only a little sidestep into cutting a dance single or two in order to keep those hits coming. Having the words 'rock 'n' roll' in a title was no barrier to sneaking in new ideas and – even if it was not recognised at the time – the opening track and first single from the new Bad Company album proved they could do it as well as anyone. Though it failed as a 45 in Britain – despite enthusiastic airplay from Tommy Vance's *Friday Rock Show* on Radio 1, and Nicky Horne's *Your Mother Wouldn't Like It* on Capital – the single gave Bad Company their final major US hit, peaking at number 13. Being their biggest-selling single in America after 'Can't Get Enough' was enough to generate sufficient interest in and subsequent sales for the album.

'Crazy Circles' – like 'Seagull' from the debut album – was a glimpse of the more laid-back, folky side of the band. Acoustic guitar and tinkling piano all fit together like a glove, to say nothing of the charming, lightly picked guitar break and soaring delicate vocal harmonies.

Boz's song 'Gone, Gone, Gone' marries a gutsy three-note guitar riff and a firm slap on the drums, providing one of the album's most infectious moments. It became a minor hit single in America later that year, reaching number 56.

'Evil Wind' has an understated current of menace. Hard-rocking with just a touch of funk about it, it culminates in a blazing lead break in the style more associated with Carlos Santana and the Latin-American rock so prevalent earlier in the decade. A contrast comes with 'Early In The Morning' – a soft, peaceful love song with predominant piano and a crystal-clear guitar solo at the end.

Side two starts with three songs written by Mick. 'Lonely For Your Love' rocks out from the start with something of a nod to 'Can't Get Enough'. It has razor-sharp guitar, a chorus built around three chords, and Paul turns on the aggression as he sings higher than usual.

'Oh, Atlanta', which has no connections with the Little Feat classic apart from a similar title. A laid-back country feel and a great harmonica break make this song a standout on the set. It's followed by 'Take The Time': an attractive mid-tempo song with some tasteful acoustic lines.

If anyone was looking for something to lift off the album and develop as a 12" club mix – like so many other rock acts – the unashamedly catchy 'Rhythm Machine' would've been bang on target. Appropriately, it was co-written by both members of the group's rhythm section, and it sounds nothing like Bad Company as their fans knew them. Granted, the lyrics are pretty clichéd: 'I'm a rhythm machine, I'm a music man/I play the blues wherever I can'. But with such a dance-floor-friendly bass line, bubbling electric keyboards (Is that a Billy Preston lick or two from 'Get Back', or am I imagining it?) and a naggingly commercial riff, it might've taken the band down a very different career path, and possibly not one they would've wanted. At one point, Paul even ad libs a spoken 'Boom boom': a sly nod to the ubiquitous syndrum sound that was used on so many disco 45s around that time. It may sound too much like pure pop by half, and completely out of character for Bad Company, but it still works in spite of that.

Finally, 'She Brings Me Love' ends the album in love song territory. It does very much bring to mind Joe Cocker's immortal version of The Beatles' 'With A Little Help From My Friends', with the three-chord organ intro followed by a steady drums build-up and touches of guitar near the beginning that recall Jimmy Page's work on Cocker's record. The song is more or less in waltz time, with soulful backing vocals built on those same three chords, and more searing guitar towards the fade.

Years later, Paul was asked about the worst review he'd ever received. He said it was for 'Rock 'n' Roll Fantasy'. The first line of the review was, 'The coffin creaks open…' He knew it was not going to be a good write-up, but said, 'You've got to try to be philosophical about it.' Other critics differed, hailing it as a return to form, even if it was some way below the standard of the first three. On both sides of the Atlantic it became another top ten album: in fact, their last.

From April to October, Bad Company toured America, selling out venues everywhere and still selling albums in quantity. Little did anyone realise that their farewell to the decade would in a sense be the band's farewell too. Not for another seven years would Bad Company appear onstage again, and by then it would be with a different vocalist.

Postscript: Sail On

Since forming in 1973, Bad Company had owed much of their success to one of the toughest managers in the business. Peter Grant always did his best for the two acts in which he believed the most, and his role in making them among the most successful acts of the 1970s could not be underestimated. In 1980, it all came to a halt. He was already starting to lose his grip, thanks to his own personal demons – notably cocaine – as Led Zeppelin's future became increasingly precarious. John Bonham's death in September 1980 not only brought the curtain down on Led Zeppelin, but dealt everyone else in the Swan Song empire a heavy blow, and three months later, the music world was shocked even more by the killing of John Lennon.

Now happily married with children, Paul wanted more of a domestic life and was finding the workload particularly onerous: 'Maybe a part of me had already sort of flown the coop.' He said the band and its music had completely overtaken his life. He told the others he wanted time away to watch the family grow up, and to record a solo album. Peter was becoming a recluse, so there was no firm management hand to guide them.

Simon said Peter had been the glue that held Bad Company together, and in his absence they came apart, feeling he'd 'abandoned the ship a little bit'. Moreover, they were 'pretty much spent as a band', exhausted, not really getting on with each other, and reluctant to go back into the studio again at all as they were struggling to find their creative force. Mick believed that Bad Company had become bigger than all of them, and to continue would've destroyed someone, or something. It might've been bad business strategy, but on balance, Paul's instinct was correct.

After a brief hiatus for several months, in the autumn of 1981, they returned to Ridge Farm Studios with another new album in mind. Before they did, Paul decided that in an attempt to return to their roots, they would play a small local village hall gig – seating capacity about 200 – calling themselves Rough Diamonds. A rumour went around that it might be Bad Company, and they attracted a cross-section of Hell's Angels, Teddy boys and local gentry. Apart from near riots outside, it went down well: despite – if not because of – so many different members of society turning up.

Despite this homely overture, prospects for the new work were not good. Paul realised they were running out of energy. He thought the others were not really pulling their weight, partying too much, enjoying the rock star life and not focusing on what they should be doing. In the studio, he became increasingly frustrated: anxious about whether they could really get it together. Under such conditions, the *Rough Diamonds* album was bound to be a disappointing coda to their career; or, in Simon's words, 'a sad way to end that version of Bad Company'. It had the air of a contractual obligation project as they all arrived with song ideas and demos, some of the material more or less ready to go, some only half-finished or less. Of the ten tracks, five were the work of Paul, one a collaboration between Paul and Simon, with two each by Mick and Boz. Paul provided lead guitar for three of the tracks.

Personal relationships between them were difficult, and on one occasion, Paul and Boz had to be physically restrained by the other two after an argument descended into physical violence. Nevertheless, Paul said far too much was made of the incident; they did have a tussle, but that was nothing new. When the dust had settled, they were still brothers in arms, fight or no fight, split or no split. They had simply overdone it, and burned themselves out in the process.

Released in August 1982, *Rough Diamonds* charted higher in Britain – reaching number 15 in its first week – than in America, where it peaked at 26. Always regarded as the runt of the litter, in retrospect it has its good points. But in all fairness – despite Paul's unmistakable vocals – it does not sound like the Bad Company of the mid-1970s. 'Electricland', which was rightly chosen as a single (in fact, the only one), reached number 74 stateside, but was not even released as a single in Britain. With its insistent rhythm and a strong hook, it stands out as the album's best three minutes. 'Untie The Knot' – the album's only collaboration – a combined effort by Paul and Simon – has quite a satisfying funky rhythm, with shades of early Doobie Brothers and a Santana-like guitar figure, developed from a chord sequence of Simon's that had soured. In view of what was happening to the band, Simon commented that the theme appeared to be rather prophetic, even though he was sure it concerned the end of a man-woman relationship.

Mel Collins plays some sterling saxophone here and there, notably on 'Nuthin' On The TV'. One of Boz's two songs, it was a halfway stab at social comment: 'All I ever hear about is ayatollahs/The headline scream and the newscast hollers'. But apart from brass fills, a funky backbeat and an element of Dr. John blues meets jazz, it fails to go anywhere. Boz's other contribution – 'Ballad Of The Band' – is enlivened by some interesting piano and sax touches, not far removed from the sound Roy Wood and

Wizzard had aimed at in their more jazz-influenced moments, but the song lacks that final punch. In fact, several of the tracks have something of a funk tinge, as if the band had been listening to Average White Band, Little Feat and others, and decided this was the path to take. The feeling is that they were looking for a more contemporary sound in the early 1980s, but lacked the interest or commitment to follow it through.

After that, Paul left the band. He was ready to come off the road and had sensed the feeling that they were just flying a little too high, getting a little too crazy, and something had to give. The deaths of Bonham and Lennon had been a further reality check – a trigger to enjoy making music at his own pace in the studio he'd built in his house, and to spend more time with his family. When he released the long-planned solo album with the significant title *Cut Loose* in October 1983, it was clearly the end for Bad Company for a while. No official announcement was made, as nobody would rule out the possibility they might get back together again, but as the years went by, it looked more unlikely.

Meanwhile, Simon joined Wildlife – a five-piece British band who released an eponymous album in 1983 on which he played drums, and saxophone on one track. Produced by Mick Ralphs, it was the last to be released on the Swan Song label before it was discontinued for new releases, to remain only as an imprint for Led Zeppelin reissues. Wildlife disbanded the following year and Simon played drums on Mick's first solo album, *Take This!*

After Paul played with several other major names from the music world – including Eric Clapton, Jeff Beck, Bill Wyman, Charlie Watts, Steve Winwood and Kenney Jones, on the A.R.M.S. (Action for Research into Multiple Sclerosis) benefit concert in 1983 (founded by Ronnie Lane, who'd suffered from the disease for several years) – he and Jimmy Page decided to work together. The following year, they formed The Firm, with Tony Franklin on bass and Chris Slade on drums. It was arguably not the best name they could've chosen, as The Firm was also a novelty outfit of 'Arthur Daley ('e's Alright)' and 'Star Trekkin'' fame, though there was little chance of one act being confused with the other. Nevertheless, they only saw themselves as a short-term project. They toured Europe and America, playing just two concerts in Britain, and released two albums – one eponymous, which hit the top 20 in 1985, and *Mean Business*: a top 50 hit one year later.

Rich Chamberlain of *Music Radar online* once asked Paul how his approach had changed and evolved when working with other guitarists later in his career. He answered that it differed only in that there were new personalities involved, as they shared a common goal in wanting to come up with finished songs. 'Tear Down The Walls' from the second album was an example where Jimmy Page had all the music and Paul wrote the lyrics: 'But one doesn't have to be famous to write with somebody. It's all about chemistry and whether or not you just click. It's about getting on the same wavelength. It's all about communication really.'

In 1986, Bad Company rose from the ashes. They had severed their managerial association with Peter Grant (now officially retired), and Swan Song was now history. The band were technically on the Atlantic label and Ahmet Ertegun contacted Mick with a view to their reforming. He and Simon started to look for a vocalist. They were unhappy with Paul's attitude and complete lack of interest; Simon saying that just because one player left the team, that was no reason for the rest to give up. As Paul was such a hard act to follow, Mick was unsure about recruiting another singer, but he could see the business advantages of doing so and retaining a tried and trusted band name. Though it could never be quite the same as before, they decided to give it a go, especially as Mick had nothing else to do at the time.

For Simon, this four-year period had been probably the worst of his life, exacerbated by drink and drugs issues. He admitted he was in a mess, and when Ertegun called to suggest regrouping without Paul, it seemed like a way out: 'It's a period of my life I'm not that proud of, but I will add a caveat – it might not have been Bad Company as most people remembered it, but we got a lot of new fans, and we did some pretty good tours.' Boz was happy to return, and on the recommendation of Mick Jones of Foreigner, they recruited singer Brian Howe and recorded and released five albums, beginning with *Fame And Fortune* in 1986, followed by *Dangerous Age* and *Holy Water* at two-year intervals. But their top 30 singles days in America were now a thing of the past, as they had long been in Britain.

Mick Ralphs was also in two minds about the new line-up, as he never thought Brian viewed it as a long-term project, feeling, 'He didn't really have that much respect for the original Bad Company.' The guitarist left for a while and was replaced by Geoff Whitehorn, who formed another link with Simon's past, as he'd formerly been guitarist with Crawler. Mick returned briefly, and second guitarist Dave 'Bucket' Colwell joined, taking over when Mick left again.

Yet Bad Company Mk II failed to gel. When he left in 1994, Brian said it had not been a difficult decision, as they were 'getting very sloppy live'. It was not 'a happy band' – with him and producer Terry Thomas tired of doing all the work while getting 'nothing but resentment from Mick and Simon'.

After Boz also left following the live album *What You Hear Is What You Get* in 1993, vocalist Robert Hart and bassist Rick Wills (formerly of Foreigner) came on board, recording the albums *Company Of Strangers* in 1995 and *Stories Told & Untold* – which included some new songs and re-recordings of earlier material – in 1996. Simon had mixed feelings about the newer post-Paul versions of the group, calling it a part of their history that he did regret, and he was glad when it all folded. He did not find Brian Howe the easiest person to get on with. Although reluctant to go into detail, he said Brian left various problems behind him, as after he left, promoters tended to book *him* as Bad Company, and the rest of the band 'had to deal with it'.

Meanwhile, Paul still pursued a partly solo career with his own band and collaborated with other high-profile names, which were bound to be no more than short-term projects. In 1991, he teamed up with drummer Kenney Jones: formerly of Small Faces, The Faces and The Who. Their new group The Law was designed to include different supporting musicians who would let Paul pursue any style he wished. They included guitarists Jim Barber (Rolling Stones, Mick Jagger solo and Ruby Turner), John Staehely (Spirit and Jo Jo Gunne), bassist Pino Palladino (bands led by Paul Young and Jools Holland), and guest guitarists Bryan Adams, David Gilmour and Chris Rea. After releasing one album – which peaked at number 61 in Britain and 126 in America – and playing a single gig at Milton Keynes Bowl, supporting ZZ Top and Bryan Adams, they went their separate ways.

Two years later, Paul was involved in two Jimi Hendrix tributes. The first was a collaboration with Steve Vai, Buddy Miles and Billy Cox from Hendrix's Band of Gypsys and the London Metropolitan Orchestra: recording 'Bold As Love' on the tribute album *From The Storm*. Later in 1993, Paul teamed up with Journey guitarist Neal Schon for a five-track EP of Hendrix songs recorded in July live at Bayfront Park, Miami, and released in November. That same year, he released a tribute to another notable guitarist – the solo album *Muddy Water Blues*, with a self-written title track and his reinterpretations of other blues classics. The players included the likes of Brian May, Jeff Beck, Gary Moore, Steve Miller,

Brian Setzer, Richie Sambora and David Gilmour. It proved to be the most successful venture of Paul's career by far, with the album reaching number nine in Britain, and the title track reaching number 45 in the singles chart.

In 1994 it was the 25th anniversary of the original Woodstock festival. Free had narrowly missed performing at the first, but this time the Paul Rodgers Rock and Blues Revue were there. It was the first time he and Andy Fraser (back on bass) had worked together since 1972. Also in the line-up were Slash and Neal Schon on guitars, and Jason Bonham on drums. A 13-song set on 14 August included songs by Free, Bad Company, Muddy Waters, Jimi Hendrix and inevitably 'All Right Now'.

Rarely staying with the same musicians for long, the following year Paul formed a new band with Jaz Lochrie on bass, Jimmy Copley on drums and Geoff Whitehorn on guitar. Over the next three years, they toured extensively in Europe, America and Britain, with a world tour in 1997 that extended as far as Japan and South America.

While this was going on, Paul's most notable work with other star names was 'Reaching Out': a ballad co-written by Don Black and Andy Hill. It came out in 1996 as a three-track CD single by Rock Therapy, comprising Paul on lead vocal, with Brian May, Andy Fairweather Low, Lulu, Sam Brown and Charlie Watts. Released with all monies going to the Nordoff Robbins Music Therapy Centre for children with special needs, it failed to chart, despite being granted a new-release spot on *Top Of The Pops,* which featured most of the ensemble live in the studio.

Meanwhile, Peter Grant died in November 1995, and all four original members attended the funeral. It was the first time since Paul's departure that they'd been together, and when Robert Plant told them firmly that it was time they reformed 'and put all these imposters to shame', they began to reconsider their position. While Paul had been glad to leave and embark on a solo career, he was always proud of what they achieved in their glory days, and was less enamoured with later seeing it 'descending into total chaos'. Atlantic contacted them soon afterwards with a view to issuing a box set or compilation with new material. Paul decided the time had come, and suggested they should record four fresh songs and book a rehearsal studio. Three of them all got on fine again, but now Boz was the odd one out. He'd moved more into jazz, playing complex runs that did not fit in well with the rest of the music, and he took an eternity to tune his bass. Moreover, he had problems with drugs and alcohol, 'and was really getting to be a loose cannon'.

Nevertheless, four new tracks were completed – 'Tracking Down A Runaway' by Paul, 'Hammer Of Love' by Paul with his future wife Cynthia Kereluk, and Mick's 'Hey Hey' and 'Ain't It Good'. With no additional keyboards or instrumentation apart from guitars, bass and drums, each song sounds like a deliberate attempt to get back to their roots: the 'Rolling Stones meet Free' vibe reviewers had so often picked up on. 'Hey Hey', with its strong chorus hook is probably the most instantly memorable, while 'Hammer Of Love' makes effective use of a stuttering guitar intro, rarely straying away from one chord, yet without flagging for a moment. They appeared in March 1999 on a new compilation double CD *The Original Bad Co Anthology*, alongside a choice of album tracks (significantly six from the debut, but only two from the unloved *Rough Diamonds*) and a few rarities. These included 'Little Miss Fortune': a mid-tempo song with prominent electric piano, in its mood redolent of 'The Stealer'; the B-side of 'Can't Get Enough', 'Whiskey Bottle', which was a rousing boogie from the B-side of 'Good Lovin' Gone Bad', and the previously unreleased 'Superstar Woman', which Paul had re-recorded for his *Cut Loose* solo debut. Finally, there was the original campfire recording of 'Do Right By Your Woman' from the *Run With The Pack* sessions.

With David Lee Roth opening for them, they played over 30 dates across America in the spring and summer, starting on 15 May 1999 at Ruth Eckerd Hall, Clearwater, Florida, and finishing at the Greek Theater, Los Angeles, on 8 August. While the shows had all been very successful, there were personal issues offstage, with the band divided into two factions. As Simon put it succinctly, he and Paul were sober, neither drinking nor smoking, and the other two *did* indulge, although Mick to a lesser extent. Even so, both pairs of musicians had their own bus. The Los Angeles concert was the last to feature the original four members. Mick then decided to step back from live work for family and health reasons, while Boz had been 'drifting apart' according to Simon, and they 'ended on bad terms'.

Though it was a relief to all when the tour finished, Paul and Simon embarked on further American dates in 2001. Dave Colwell and Rick Wills rejoined for several dates co-headlining with Styx and Billy Squier. Paul admitted it was no longer the same without two of the original team, but contractual commitments had to be met. Afterwards, he returned to his solo career, though as one of the most respected British rock and blues vocalists, it was inevitable that he would be invited to collaborate or participate in other people's projects.

The popularity of the CD was now at its height, with groups, artists and producers raiding vaults for outtakes, demos and previously unreleased songs to add as bonus tracks on reissued and remastered albums. Often there was enough for expansive, beautifully collated and annotated box sets as well. Free's turn came in 2000 with the arrival of *Songs of Yesterday* – a long-form box containing five CDs and a lavish booklet with complete sessionology, details about the history of every track, and a fine selection of photographs, including overseas picture sleeves and memorabilia. Of the 80 tracks, most had never been released, although some were alternative or new stereo mixes of familiar songs. The first three discs comprised studio material, including previously unheard curios like the fragmentary 'Long Tall Sally' from 1968; the first recorded version of 'All Right Now' opening with an a cappella chorus; a full unedited 'The Stealer' lasting almost four and a half minutes, and a rehearsal of 'Honky Tonk Women'. Disc four comprised 14 live tracks from the Sunderland and Croydon shows taped in 1970, 12 appearing for the first time. The fifth disc contained associated recordings by Peace, Sharks, Paul Kossoff with John Martyn, and Kossoff, Kirke, Tetsu, Rabbit, plus '(I Just Wanna) See You Smile' recorded in Jamaica in 1972 by Paul and The Maytals, and an 18-minute version of 'Time Spent (Time Away)' by Koss and John Martyn from November 1971.

Universal Music – who had acquired the Island catalogue – contacted the surviving band members for their input. Paul had mixed feelings about the release of such a collection, as any delving into unissued archive material 'can mean junk if you're not careful'. He admitted it made interesting listening for hard-core fans, and there were several outtakes that he'd completely forgotten about. The Maytals track – that he had long assumed was completely lost – 'was quite refreshing to hear'. Andy was less enthusiastic, telling Paul that he was singing on some numbers and it sounded like he was 12 years old. 'Give me a break.'

Although he'd always distanced himself from any politics or controversy in his lyrics, in September 2002, Paul accepted an invitation from Prime Minister Tony Blair to perform at the Labour Party conference. A long-time fan and briefly a member of a rock band in his student days, Blair had said during his early days in parliament that if he'd had a voice like Paul, he would never have entered politics. Paul had every member of the party in attendance singing along to 'Wishing Well', with its refrain of 'Love in a peaceful world'. He hoped the words would sink in, and later thought it ironic that it happened on the eve of going to war against Iraq: 'We shouldn't be there and I don't know why we are.'

It said much for Paul's versatility as a vocalist that he was equally at home in blues, rock and soul concerts. In February 2004, he joined bassist Billy Cox and drummer Mitch Mitchell – both of whom had worked with Jimi Hendrix – and guitarists including Joe Satriani and Buddy Guy, for three American shows in Seattle, Portland and San Francisco, billed as Experience Hendrix. When the three surviving members of The Four Tops held a 50th anniversary concert celebration at the Detroit Opera House five months later, Paul was among the select few performers they personally invited to join them onstage, in addition to Mary Wilson of The Supremes, Dennis Edwards and The Temptations Revue, Aretha Franklin, Sam Moore and Ashford & Simpson. Paul's 'Loving You Is Sweeter Than Ever' was one of the highlights, even though (according to some comments posted on an online forum afterwards) many of the audience were familiar with the Motown singers, but had no idea who Paul Rodgers was. That autumn at Wembley, he appeared at a 50th anniversary celebration for the Fender Stratocaster, alongside Brian May, David Gilmour, Ronnie Wood, Gary Moore and Joe Walsh.

Another onstage appearance that year resulted in a collaboration that lasted several years and went around the world. In November, Queen were among the first acts inducted into the new (and short-lived) UK Music Hall of Fame. At the awards ceremony, Paul as vocalist joined Brian May and Roger Taylor, playing 'We Will Rock You', 'We Are The Champions' and 'All Right Now'. In an online interview with *Vintage Rock*, Paul said that at first it seemed like just another superstar jam session, ending with the usual 'Oh yeah, we gotta do something. I'll see you later, man.' He thought that was it until Brian phoned him later and asked if he fancied doing a small tour with them in Europe, as Queen plus Paul Rodgers. Paul was amazed, thinking it might've led to their writing a few songs and playing a handful of shows for fun. Instead, he found himself part of a venture that grew from a European tour into a lengthy worldwide jaunt.

Queen + Paul Rodgers, as they billed themselves, were eager to stress that Paul was not replacing the inimitable Freddie Mercury, as their styles had been quite different. But Paul's ability to sing hard rock and ballads equally well went without saying. A setlist was devised of largely Queen songs, plus a few Free and Bad Company classics, and Rock Therapy's 'Reaching Out'. Some commentators found them an unlikely combination, with Terry Staunton of *Record Collector* opining it was 'hard to imagine Paul Rodgers landing any further from his no-nonsense

Brit-blues roots'. Nevertheless, for over three and a half years on and off, they toured much of the universe, with a repertoire that changed slightly over time, and most of the dates sold out. The first show was at Brixton Academy on 28 March 2005, and the last at José Amalfitani Stadium, Buenos Aires, on 29 November 2008.

One of the first shows – at Hallam FM Arena in Sheffield – was recorded and released in 2005 as the live double CD *Return of the Champions*, hitting number 12 in Britain and 84 in America. Three years later to the month, it was followed by a studio album featuring new material written by the three musicians as individuals. *The Cosmos Rocks* was a number five hit in Britain and reached number 47 in America, though the single 'C-lebrity' – written by Roger Taylor – only hit number 33 in Britain. Any new album featuring Queen could hardly fail to reach the British top ten, but it attracted plenty of negative reviews on release. Roger admitted afterwards that while Paul was one of their favourite singers ever, being a blues and soul man, he was not the perfect frontman for them. Roger was also angry that EMI – who were going through major troubles at the time – lost sales by not promoting the album properly. He found that several record shops in Europe were not stocking it though Queen were touring there at the time, and he sometimes wondered why they ever made the record.

The partnership did not occupy all of Paul's time at this point, and in December 2007, he was one of the supporting acts for what was one of the most long-awaited band reformations in rock history. A benefit concert in memory of Ahmet Ertegun – who had died the previous year – was announced for the O2 Arena in London, to be headlined by Led Zeppelin, who were reforming strictly for the occasion, with John Bonham's son Jason on drums. Over 20,000,000 requests were received for the 20,000 (or less) tickets available to the public, making it the most over-subscribed gig of all time. Paul and his band – plus a band consisting of Keith Emerson with Simon Kirke and members of Yes, and Bill Wyman's Rhythm Kings – were among the opening acts.

Paul had greatly enjoyed the 'hugely challenging' experience of working with Queen, as never before had he joined an established band with a whole repertoire as well as a reputation. But it was never meant to be a permanent arrangement, and in May 2009, they announced that their musical partnership had officially come to an end, though 'the door remained open'.

Meanwhile, as Paul and Queen were drawing the crowds, there were two versions of his previous band playing without him. In May 2007,

Robert Hart, Dave Colwell and Jaz Lochrie performed in a pub at Surbiton to raise funds for the Macmillan Cancer Trust. Performing as Rock and Roll Fantasy, they offered a show of Bad Company songs for an audience of a few hundred, and were joined by Mick Ralphs with Chris Grainger on drums. One year later, an identical line-up – except for Gary 'Harry' James on drums – toured under the name of Mick Ralphs' Bad Company.

The most lasting result of this temporary alliance was a phone call from the band's lawyers that spurred Paul and Simon into another reunion. Simon said nothing had been done to perpetuate their trademark, and if after ten years this was not addressed, 'someone can grab it'. They needed to do a show: 'It was as simple and mercenary as that.' (They also needed to reclaim their name, after an English drum-and-bass-led group of the same name appeared in 1998, and were obliged to rebrand themselves as Bad Company UK or simply BC to avoid confusion.) In Paul's words, it was necessary to 'protect the legacy they have built and cement the rights to the trademark Bad Company for touring'. Fortunately, after such a long time apart, they all got on extremely well. The remaining three – accompanied by former Heart guitarist Howard Leese and bassist Lynn Sorensen – regrouped, and after two days of rehearsal, they played a one-off gig at the Seminole Hard Rock Hotel & Casino in Hollywood, Florida. Seventeen Bad Company songs were played that night, and Paul dedicated 'Gone, Gone, Gone' to Boz Burrell, who had succumbed to a heart attack (or maybe an aneurysm, according to his wife Cathy) at his home in Spain on 21 September 2006. It was the ultimate rock 'n' roll passing. At a large buffet garden party thrown to celebrate Boz's sixtieth birthday, he borrowed a guitar to show somebody the chords to a song, dropped the instrument and collapsed lifeless on the ground. As Mick commented afterwards, it was surely the way he would've wanted to go.

A Bad Company in concert recording *Hard Rock Live* was released on CD and DVD in 2010. Throughout 2009 and 2010, the new five-piece line-up played further shows in America, Britain and Japan. Mick had to pull out of the Japanese dates as he was undergoing hip replacement surgery, leaving Howard to take on guitar duties alone.

Having completed commitments with Queen, in 2009, Paul was offered the chance to step into the shoes of another established band member. Aerosmith guitarist Joe Perry had told him that Steven Tyler was not keen to take part in their forthcoming tour, and asked Paul to join on a temporary basis. Paul was reluctant, and when Steve returned to the fold, Paul said it was the right decision for them. He declined, as he'd already done something similar with Queen, although he was quick to point out that they were an exception in that he'd joined forces with an actual band (or the core of it) that already existed. In the past, he had always formed a band and then written a catalogue of songs for them, but now he was disinclined to go down that road a second time.

In May 2011, Paul received one of the ultimate accolades: an Ivor Novello award in recognition of his 'Outstanding contribution to British music'. Two years later, a project long dear to his heart – and another of the highlights of his solo career – was realised with the recording of *The Royal Sessions* at Royal Studios in Memphis in 2013. Released early the following year, it comprised his versions of old blues and soul standards, including 'Walk On By', 'I Can't Stand The Rain', 'I've Been Loving You Too Long' and 'Born Under a Bad Sign': songs that inspired him in younger days. All proceeds would go to the Stax Music Academy after-school music programme in Memphis, so he could help 'pay the proceeds to the people who gave us this music'.

Bad Company continued to endure at various stages throughout the next decade, with a changing personnel as ever, while their vocalist and drummer remained the two constants. In June 2012, Todd Ronning from Paul's solo band took over bass when they played a Swedish rock festival: the first date they'd done in mainland Europe for over 30 years. But the original band that had started it all, was not forgotten. That summer, Paul, Simon and Andy Fraser were invited to join a line-up of British acts, with another guitarist of their choice, to play 'All Right Now' at the ceremony that closed the London Olympic Games. The obvious one to complete the quartet would've been Brian May, but they declined to play the gig at all, no matter who would have been on guitar. As Paul had often stated, the story of Free started and ended with Paul Kossoff.

Andy Fraser's musical activities in the last few years of his life were curtailed by ill health, after being diagnosed with HIV and then a rare form of cancer. He died on 16 March 2015 at his home in California, aged 62.

For Bad Company, live dates on the same bill as other major performers from the 1970s continued, albeit on a fitful basis. In March 2013, they announced a joint 40th anniversary tour with Lynyrd Skynyrd – 1973 having been the year of the American band's first album and the British act's formation. Paul loved the experience, saying, 'It was like the old days, but we were sober!' It was so successful that a similar jaunt for both units took place the following year.

In 2016 they embarked on an American tour with Joe Walsh, but by this time, Mick Ralphs – now aged 70 – was having to curtail *his* activities for health reasons. He didn't take part in this tour and Rich Robinson of the Black Crowes stepped in, although Mick was well enough to rejoin the band in June for a UK arena tour with Richie Sambora, culminating in a show at London's O2 Arena in October. The curtain came down on Mick's band days later that year, after he took part in a Mott The Hoople reunion and was hospitalised shortly after the last show, having suffered a stroke that made it unlikely he would play guitar again.

Further touring came in 2017 for Paul and Simon with Howard Leese on guitar and Todd Ronning on bass, and another union with Lynyrd Skynyrd for The Last of the Street Survivors tour in 2018. Also in May 2017, Paul undertook the 'Free Spirit' tour of Britain, performing songs from the Free back catalogue, culminating in a show at the Royal Albert Hall recorded for CD and DVD release the following year. By the time of his 70th birthday, in December 2019, he could look back on a remarkably varied career spanning over half a century, with two successive iconic bands of the late 1960s and 1970s, and solo and collaborative ventures thereafter in several music genres. In the process, he'd also participated in several concerts for good causes and charities dear to his heart. Throughout the years, one of the most unmistakable and well-respected vocalists ever to come out of Britain had endured, and looked set to do so for some time yet.

Brian Howe died on 6 May 2020, aged 66. To minimise any confusion, Paul posted a video on social media to confirm he was still very much alive and well. For the surviving original and newer members of Bad Company, occasional tours and gigs looked set to continue as long as the demand was there and as long as they were still fit and well enough to play them. But their career in regard to writing and recording fresh material seemingly came to an end in 1998 with the four tracks for *Anthology*. While Simon was enthusiastic about returning to the studio sometime in the future, Paul was less interested. In 2014, he told interviewer Kevin Murphy in *Classic Rock*, that there were no plans for them to make another album. While he still felt a great deal of passion for his craft and was still writing all the time, he said music was moving him 'in other directions'. Jon Brewer – who directed and produced a 40th anniversary DVD on the band that year, said he thought they needed 'to show more consistency' if they were to confirm their claim to being one of the giants of rock. That included more touring, as opposed to just the occasional collection of dates. The problem that faced them was what they would write about if they were to come up with new songs. Who would want to buy them? The kids who'd just discovered them and adored the old albums, or the older fans who would still buy tickets to come and see them but might not be interested in buying a new CD? A few years later, they could have also argued that those same fans could stream everything they wanted without having to buy. Simon realised that times had changed so much since the release of their debut album in 1974, and after 40 years or more, he was no longer sure that – much as he would love to go back into the studio – they could justify another album. Classic rock, sadly (or any music, in fact), no longer sold well anymore, even if by 2019/20 the likes of Deep Purple, The Who and Status Quo could still enter the British top ten with new albums in the first week of release.

At the same time, not long before he was sidelined by ill health, Mick Ralphs summed up their 40 years (and counting) history with the reflection that at the band's heart was a simple love of unpretentious blues rock. The music came first, regardless of the fashions of the day, and he found it incredible that 40 years after the first album, it was still attracting new fans. Mick said that watching Jon Brewer's DVD brought tears to his eyes – not because he was an old romantic, but because it brought back so many memories. What he loved about Bad Company was that none of it was ever planned, but 'made up as we went along'. Forty years after getting together as a band for the first time, the three surviving original members could look back on everything and still smile about it – they were, in fact, very *good* company after all.

Simon had the distinction of being the only constant member, having played drums at every Bad Company gig over more than 40 years. When interviewer Henry Yates from *Classic Rock* asked Simon about the chances of future live work, he answered that it was a question of 'How long have we got left?' They still sounded good together – with the pettiness, the business of falling out with each other, splitting up and doing their own thing, all now a thing of the past: 'It's just time to play the music for the music's sake. There's still a spark between us all, and it's a very big spark.' As the lyrics from their theme song from the debut album went: 'Bad Company, 'til the day I die'.

Resources

Books

Clayton, D., Smith, T.K., *Heavy Load: Free* (Moonshine, 2000)
Fraser, A., Hughes, M., *All Right Now: Life, Death, and Life Again* (Foruli Codex, 2015)
Garner, K., *The Peel Sessions* (BBC, 2007)
Gillan, I., Cohen, D., *Ian Gillan: The Autobiography of Deep Purple's Lead Singer* (Blake, 1998)
Humphries, P., *Top of the Pops 50th Anniversary* (McNidder & Grace, 2013)
James, J., *Paul Kossoff: All Right Now: The Guitars, the Gear, the Music* (Matador, 2017)
Rosen, S., *Free at Last: The Story of Free and Bad Company* (SAF, 2001)
Shapiro, H., *Alexis Korner: The Biography* (Bloomsbury, 1996)
Wall, M., *When Giants Walked the Earth: 50 Years of Led Zeppelin* (Trapeze, 2020)

Articles and Interviews

Barton, G., *'Freddie would love it…' (Queen + Paul Rodgers)* (Classic Rock, May 2005)
Brown, G., *'Straight Shooters'* (Melody Maker, 3 May 1975)
Charlesworth, C., *'Four into Free won't go'* (Melody Maker, 3 July 1971)
Elliott, P., *'Paul Rodgers: "My greatest regret is not having Paul Kossoff around."'* (Classic Rock, August 2016)
Heatley, M., *'1970: Best of times, worst of times'* (Classic Rock, May 2005)
Kent, N., *'…Well, come on then, Rodgers, act mean and nasty for the kids!'* (NME, 17 January 1976)
Rosen, S., *'Free at Last'* (Classic Rock, May 2005)
Scoppa, B., *'Dark and stormy delight'* (review of *Bad Company*) (Rolling Stone, 29 August 1974)
Valentine, P., *'Bad Company: Desolation Angels have gastric juices, too'* (Creem, June 1979)
Various, *'Bad Company Collector's Pack'* (special issue magazine including several articles and DVD) (Classic Rock, 2014)
Wall, M., *'Bad Company: The bad old days'* (Classic Rock, May 2014); *'Rock Steady'* (Classic Rock, March 2014)
Walsh, J., *'Paul Rodgers: He will rock you'* (Independent, 23 October 2011)

Walters, I., *'The way they choose'* (Let It Rock, March 1975)
Welch, C., *'Jogging back to happiness'* (Melody Maker, 31 March 1979)

Internet

Chamberlain, R., *'It was such a great band because Paul Kossoff was such a great guitar player'* (Music Radar online, 2014)
Pemberton, P., *'Paul Rodgers says John Bonham's death influenced decision to quit Bad Company'* (spinner.com, 27 August 2010)
vintagerock.com
allmusic.com
Discogs.com
45cat.com vinyl database

On Track series

Alan Parsons Project – Steve Swift
978-1-78952-154-2
Tori Amos – Lisa Torem 978-1-78952-142-9
Asia – Peter Braidis 978-1-78952-099-6
Badfinger – Robert Day-Webb
978-1-878952-176-4
Barclay James Harvest – Keith and Monica Domone
978-1-78952-067-5
The Beatles – Andrew Wild 978-1-78952-009-5
The Beatles Solo 1969-1980 – Andrew Wild
978-1-78952-030-9
Blue Oyster Cult – Jacob Holm-Lupo
978-1-78952-007-1
Blur – Matt Bishop 978-178952-164-1
Marc Bolan and T.Rex – Peter Gallagher
978-1-78952-124-5
Kate Bush – Bill Thomas 978-1-78952-097-2
Camel – Hamish Kuzminski 978-1-78952-040-8
Caravan – Andy Boot 978-1-78952-127-6
Cardiacs – Eric Benac 978-1-78952-131-3
Eric Clapton Solo – Andrew Wild
978-1-78952-141-2
The Clash – Nick Assirati 978-1-78952-077-4
Crosby, Stills and Nash – Andrew Wild
978-1-78952-039-2
The Damned – Morgan Brown
978-1-78952-136-8
Deep Purple and Rainbow 1968-79 –
Steve Pilkington 978-1-78952-002-6
Dire Straits – Andrew Wild 978-1-78952-044-6
The Doors – Tony Thompson
978-1-78952-137-5
Dream Theater – Jordan Blum
978-1-78952-050-7
Electric Light Orchestra – Barry Delve
978-1-78952-152-8
Elvis Costello and The Attractions –
Georg Purvis 978-1-78952-129-0
Emerson Lake and Palmer – Mike Goode
978-1-78952-000-2
Fairport Convention – Kevan Furbank
978-1-78952-051-4
Peter Gabriel – Graeme Scarfe
978-1-78952-138-2
Genesis – Stuart MacFarlane 978-1-78952-005-7
Gentle Giant – Gary Steel 978-1-78952-058-3
Gong – Kevan Furbank 978-1-78952-082-8
Hall and Oates – Ian Abrahams
978-1-78952-167-2
Hawkwind – Duncan Harris 978-1-78952-052-1
Peter Hammill – Richard Rees Jones
978-1-78952-163-4
Roy Harper – Opher Goodwin
978-1-78952-130-6
Jimi Hendrix – Emma Stott 978-1-78952-175-7
The Hollies – Andrew Darlington
978-1-78952-159-7
Iron Maiden – Steve Pilkington
978-1-78952-061-3
Jefferson Airplane – Richard Butterworth
978-1-78952-143-6
Jethro Tull – Jordan Blum 978-1-78952-016-3
Elton John in the 1970s – Peter Kearns
978-1-78952-034-7
The Incredible String Band – Tim Moon
978-1-78952-107-8
Iron Maiden – Steve Pilkington
978-1-78952-061-3
Judas Priest – John Tucker 978-1-78952-018-7
Kansas – Kevin Cummings 978-1-78952-057-6
The Kinks – Martin Hutchinson
978-1-78952-172-6
Korn – Matt Karpe 978-1-78952-153-5
Led Zeppelin – Steve Pilkington
978-1-78952-151-1
Level 42 – Matt Philips 978-1-78952-102-3
Little Feat – 978-1-78952-168-9
Aimee Mann – Jez Rowden 978-1-78952-036-1
Joni Mitchell – Peter Kearns 978-1-78952-081-1
The Moody Blues – Geoffrey Feakes
978-1-78952-042-2
Motorhead – Duncan Harris 978-1-78952-173-3
Mike Oldfield – Ryan Yard 978-1-78952-060-6
Opeth – Jordan Blum 978-1-78-952-166-5
Tom Petty – Richard James 978-1-78952-128-3
Porcupine Tree – Nick Holmes
978-1-78952-144-3
Queen – Andrew Wild 978-1-78952-003-3
Radiohead – William Allen 978-1-78952-149-8
Renaissance – David Detmer 978-1-78952-062-0
The Rolling Stones 1963-80 – Steve Pilkington 978-1-78952-017-0
The Smiths and Morrissey –
Tommy Gunnarsson 978-1-78952-140-5
Status Quo the Frantic Four Years –
Richard James 978-1-78952-160-3
Steely Dan – Jez Rowden 978-1-78952-043-9
Steve Hackett – Geoffrey Feakes
978-1-78952-098-9
Thin Lizzy – Graeme Stroud 978-1-78952-064-4
Toto – Jacob Holm-Lupo 978-1-78952-019-4
U2 – Eoghan Lyng 978-1-78952-078-1
UFO – Richard James 978-1-78952-073-6
The Who – Geoffrey Feakes
978-1-78952-076-7

Roy Wood and the Move – James R Turner 978-1-78952-008-8
Van Der Graaf Generator – Dan Coffey 978-1-78952-031-6
Yes – Stephen Lambe 978-1-78952-001-9
Frank Zappa 1966 to 1979 – Eric Benac 978-1-78952-033-0
Warren Zevon – Peter Gallagher 978-1-78952-170-2
10CC – Peter Kearns 978-1-78952-054-5

Decades Series

The Bee Gees in the 1960s – Andrew Mon Hughes et al 978-1-78952-148-1
The Bee Gees in the 1970s – Andrew Mon Hughes et al 978-1-78952-179-5
Black Sabbath in the 1970s – Chris Sutton 978-1-78952-171-9
Britpop – Peter Richard Adams and Matt Pooler 978-1-78952-169-6
Alice Cooper in the 1970s – Chris Sutton 978-1-78952-104-7
Curved Air in the 1970s – Laura Shenton 978-1-78952-069-9
Bob Dylan in the 1980s – Don Klees 978-1-78952-157-3
Fleetwood Mac in the 1970s – Andrew Wild 978-1-78952-105-4
Focus in the 1970s – Stephen Lambe 978-1-78952-079-8
Free and Bad Company in the 1970s – John Van der Kiste 978-1-78952-178-8
Genesis in the 1970s – Bill Thomas 978178952-146-7
George Harrison in the 1970s – Eoghan Lyng 978-1-78952-174-0
Marillion in the 1980s – Nathaniel Webb 978-1-78952-065-1
Mott the Hoople and Ian Hunter in the 1970s – John Van der Kiste 978-1-78-952-162-7
Pink Floyd In The 1970s – Georg Purvis 978-1-78952-072-9
Tangerine Dream in the 1970s – Stephen Palmer 978-1-78952-161-0
The Sweet in the 1970s – Darren Johnson 978-1-78952-139-9
Uriah Heep in the 1970s – Steve Pilkington 978-1-78952-103-0
Yes in the 1980s – Stephen Lambe with David Watkinson 978-1-78952-125-2

On Screen series

Carry On… – Stephen Lambe 978-1-78952-004-0
David Cronenberg – Patrick Chapman 978-1-78952-071-2
Doctor Who: The David Tennant Years – Jamie Hailstone 978-1-78952-066-8
James Bond – Andrew Wild – 978-1-78952-010-1
Monty Python – Steve Pilkington 978-1-78952-047-7
Seinfeld Seasons 1 to 5 – Stephen Lambe 978-1-78952-012-5

Other Books

1967: A Year In Psychedelic Rock – Kevan Furbank 978-1-78952-155-9
1970: A Year In Rock – John Van der Kiste 978-1-78952-147-4
1973: The Golden Year of Progressive Rock 978-1-78952-165-8
Babysitting A Band On The Rocks – G.D. Praetorius 978-1-78952-106-1
Eric Clapton Sessions – Andrew Wild 978-1-78952-177-1
Derek Taylor: For Your Radioactive Children – Andrew Darlington 978-1-78952-038-5
The Golden Road: The Recording History of The Grateful Dead – John Kilbride 978-1-78952-156-6
Iggy and The Stooges On Stage 1967-1974 – Per Nilsen 978-1-78952-101-6
Jon Anderson and the Warriors – the road to Yes – David Watkinson 978-1-78952-059-0
Nu Metal: A Definitive Guide – Matt Karpe 978-1-78952-063-7
Tommy Bolin: In and Out of Deep Purple – Laura Shenton 978-1-78952-070-5
Maximum Darkness – Deke Leonard 978-1-78952-048-4
Maybe I Should've Stayed In Bed – Deke Leonard 978-1-78952-053-8
The Twang Dynasty – Deke Leonard 978-1-78952-049-1

and many more to come!

Would you like to write for Sonicbond Publishing?

At Sonicbond Publishing we are always on the look-out for authors, particularly for our two main series:

On Track. Mixing fact with in depth analysis, the On Track series examines the work of a particular musical artist or group. All genres are considered from easy listening and jazz to 60s soul to 90s pop, via rock and metal.

On Screen. This series looks at the world of film and television. Subjects considered include directors, actors and writers, as well as entire television and film series. As with the On Track series, we balance fact with analysis.

While professional writing experience would, of course, be an advantage the most important qualification is to have real enthusiasm and knowledge of your subject. First-time authors are welcomed, but the ability to write well in English is essential.

Sonicbond Publishing has distribution throughout Europe and North America, and all books are also published in E-book form. Authors will be paid a royalty based on sales of their book.

Further details are available from www.sonicbondpublishing.co.uk. To contact us, complete the contact form there or email info@sonicbondpublishing.co.uk